Discovering Jewish Meditation

SECOND EDITION

Discovering Jewish Meditation

SECOND EDITION

Instruction & Guidance for Learning an Ancient Spiritual Practice

Nan Fink Gefen, PhD

JEWISH LIGHTS Publishing
Woodstock, Vermont

Discovering Jewish Meditation, Second Edition:
Instruction & Guidance for Learning an Ancient Spiritual Practice

2011 Quality Paperback Edition, First Printing

Library of Congress Cataloging-in-Publication Data

Gefen, Nan Fink.
Discovering Jewish meditation : instruction & guidance for learning an ancient spiritual practice / Nan Fink Gefen. — 2nd ed.
p. cm.
Includes bibliographical references.
ISBN 978-1-58023-462-7 (quality pbk.)
1. Jewish meditations. 2. Meditation—Judaism. 3. Spiritual life—Judaism.
I. Title.
BM724.G44 2011
296.7'2—dc22
2011016125

Second Edition
10 9 8 7 6 5 4 3 2 1
Manufactured in the United States of America

Cover art © Karol Kozlowski. Image from BigStockPhoto.com, modified by Gloria Todt
Cover design: Gloria Todt
Text design: Sans Serif, Inc.

Published by Jewish Lights Publishing
A Division of LongHill Partners, Inc.
Sunset Farm Offices, Route 4, P.O. Box 237
Woodstock, Vermont 05091
Tel: (802) 457-4000 Fax: (802) 457-4004
www.jewishlights.com

Contents

Introduction to the Second Edition

In the first edition of *Discovering Jewish Meditation* (Jewish Lights Publishing), I began this introduction by saying that Jewish meditation is a profound spiritual practice. In this second edition, I underscore that statement.

Jewish meditation is a practice that can sustain you and deepen your connection to the Divine over the course of your lifetime. Seekers throughout history have practiced it and reaped its rewards, and today many people are making it a significant part of their everyday spiritual practice.

I am one of those people. I depend on meditation to keep my mind calm, my thoughts clear, and my connection to the Holy vibrant and strong.

I discovered Jewish meditation by chance more than twenty-five years ago. I was reading books about Jewish mysticism, and I came across references to meditation within the Jewish tradition. This surprised me since I thought that Judaism was a pragmatic, in-this-world religion rather than one that can lead to spiritual transformation. I'd always assumed that meditation was part of other traditions, not mine.

Intrigued, I began to investigate. My limited knowledge of Hebrew precluded me from diving into esoteric Hebrew texts, and the English texts that were available had little guidance in starting a spiritual practice of Jewish meditation. Without a guide, I couldn't figure out how Jewish meditation was done or whether anyone was still doing it. Nevertheless, I was determined to find a way into it.

At that time, I yearned to cultivate a spiritual practice that would infuse my daily existence with meaning. I was struggling with some personal issues, and I had hope that meditation would help me find deeper wisdom and a sense of peace.

I began slowly. Every morning I set aside twenty minutes to meditate. I simply observed my breath, noticing the rise and fall of my chest and the feelings in my body. It didn't take long for me to discover that my mind had a mind of its own—even though I intended to stay focused on my breath, it kept wandering from thought to thought, out of control. After a lot of practice, I learned to let go of each thought as it arose and return to the starting point of breath.

When I felt secure in my ability to do this simple meditation, I tried others. I experimented with the meditations in this book, which I learned from colleagues or discovered myself through reading and experience. I developed a core practice of familiar meditations, sometimes going for months with the *Hineini* meditation, the first I teach in this book, or one of the others. I tried meditating at different times of the day and in different settings, experiencing the effect of subtle energies on my practice.

The results of this practice amazed me. I can say with conviction that Jewish meditation transformed my life. I became steadier, more aware, and more focused. I experienced a deeper connection to the presence of the Holy in everything around me. Meditation didn't make the issues in my life go away, but I saw them through a different lens and found that I was handling them in more fruitful ways.

As my Jewish meditation practice became central to my

spiritual well-being, I began to teach others how to do it. I did this carefully and with humility, knowing I was only a few steps ahead of my students. I learned an enormous amount from them through the questions they asked and the accounts of their experience. For twelve years, my main work was teaching Jewish meditation and Jewish spiritual practice at Chochmat HaLev, a center of Jewish meditation in the Bay Area. During that time, we trained almost a hundred people from around the U.S. to become Jewish meditation teachers; many of these people are doing this work now in their own communities.

As I write this introduction to the second edition, Jewish meditation has moved closer to becoming a mainstream practice in the Jewish world. It is no longer seen as not-Jewish, or a fringe activity, or a threatening esoteric practice. I seldom hear the statement that was once so familiar: "There's no such thing as Jewish meditation." Many synagogues and JCCs now offer classes on Jewish meditation, and it's not so unusual for meditations to be introduced into services.

This is good news for you, the reader.

Chances are that you won't be alone as you begin to learn the practice of Jewish meditation. Hopefully you'll find a class to take, or a group to join, or other meditators around you or in your community. If not, you can use this book to learn how to practice. At the very least, you'll know that many people are doing this practice in the U.S. and elsewhere.

Discovering Jewish Meditation is written to help you establish a Jewish meditation practice. Within its pages you will find the necessary guidance and support to do so. This book is meant to be used by Jews and interested non-Jews; people who are religious and those who aren't; those who have meditated in other traditions and those who have never meditated before. In short, it's a resource for anyone who wants to learn about the practice and embark on the path of becoming a meditator.

Part One, "The Practice of Jewish Meditation," answers frequently asked questions about meditation. It provides background information about the practice, including its history and its relationship to other meditative traditions. It also gives you detailed instructions about setting up a practice. At the end of the chapters in this section, you will find short breathing exercises to help prepare you for the core meditations in part two.

Part Two, "The Core Meditations," teaches thirteen simple meditations. You'll begin with the *hineini* meditation and then continue with focused, awareness, and emptiness meditations. All of these meditations have been practiced by large numbers of beginners, so I am comfortable recommending them to you.

In Part Three, "A Meditative Life," I look at the challenges that emerge once a meditative practice has been started, and I suggest ways to work with them. I also discuss how Jewish meditation can be combined with other Jewish spiritual practices, such as Shabbat.

In Chapter 11, a new addition to Part Three of this second edition, I provide a description of a morning meditative prayer practice, based on the traditional prayer service. Here you will see an example of how to bring meditation into your prayer life.

In this book, I stay with what I know firsthand rather than try to transmit others' ideas and techniques. My style of teaching reflects my experience with a wide variety of students, Jewish and non-Jewish, secular and religious. I write this book as a woman, recognizing that my entry into the once-male world of Jewish meditation is possible because of the insights and actions of others before me. I am grateful to those courageous people who opened the doors through which I pass.

A word about God-language in this book: I do not use the word "God" because it's a stumbling block for many readers. If asked if they believe in God, many would say no—but if asked if they have a sense of the Holy in all being, most would say yes. Likewise, I have chosen to use androgynous God-names, such as "the Holy" and "the Divine," rather than the more common masculine *Adonai* or the more feminine *Shekhinah.* These androgynous God-names, like all others, cannot express the essence of the indefinable, but at least they include both genders.

Before beginning this book, please take a moment to reflect on your expectations about Jewish meditation. If you are hoping to find the perfect practice, you will be disappointed. Like any other spiritual system, Jewish meditation has inconsistencies and conceptual gaps. It is not a neat, tidy package. My approach is to explore its richness, help you establish a practice, and name the difficulties when they appear.

Now, take a few more moments and consider your expectations for yourself as a meditator. If you demand self-perfection, you are bound to get discouraged. Nobody is a perfect meditator. Perfection isn't even a category in this practice. All meditators, including the most experienced, have their "down" times when they don't meditate or they slide off course. The important thing is to be committed to the path so that you notice when this happens—and begin to meditate again.

In other words, put aside the judge in yourself.

Some of you will read this book and practice the meditations with great enthusiasm. Others will be more irregular, trying out a meditation then stopping for a while before resuming. There isn't one approach that works for everybody. Each of us has to learn to meditate at our own pace, calibrating the amount of information or experience we absorb.

I suggest you flip through the book first so that you become familiar with the layout of the contents. Then go back and read the background material about Jewish meditation in Part One. Once you do that, you're ready to begin the first meditation in Part Two, *Hineini.* Go slow. Remember the story of the tortoise and the hare: The steady pace of the tortoise was more effective in the end than the speed of the hare.

Keep this book close to you, in a special place. You'll want to refer to it often as you learn to meditate since it is impossible to absorb all of it in one sitting.

This book will teach you how to meditate alone, which is an essential part of the practice for everyone. But consider meditating with others, when and if you can. Meditating in a group will enhance your discipline, and you'll find it rewarding to share your experience and to hear other people's ideas.

It helps to have a teacher when you have questions or difficulties. I've included a list of resources at the end of this book. But if you don't find a teacher, you still can learn to meditate by yourself. I did, and so have a great many others. You don't need a guru to tell you what to do or to guide you along the path. This book will suffice.

Above all, it is important to trust your own experience. Each of us is the best judge of our meditative process. This book offers a wide variety of meditations, and some will resonate with you. Others will be unsuitable or unappealing at this time. Let them go. Your practice of Jewish meditation will, I hope, be with you for the rest of your life, and you will have plenty of time to refine and develop it in the future.

This book is a beginning. As you develop your practice in the months and years ahead, you will enrich it with your own perceptions and experiences. The material here is meant to help you start on your journey. May it be as rich and meaningful as it has been for me.

Nan Fink Gefen, PhD

Acknowledgments

I wish to thank Stuart M. Matlins, the publisher of Jewish Lights, for his strong interest in Jewish meditation and his encouragement of this work.

I also thank Arthur Magida, Sandra Korinchak, Emily Wichland (second edition), and Daniela Cockwill (second edition), Jewish Lights editors, for their help in refining the text of this book. Their editorial expertise and support were very much appreciated.

The Jewish Lights editorial staff, including Jennifer Goneau and Martha McKinney, were a pleasure to work with as they guided me through the prepublication stages.

Through the years, I have learned a great deal about Jewish meditation from many teachers and colleagues. Among them are Sylvia Boorstein, David and Shoshana Cooper, Avram Davis, Shefa Gold, Alan Lew (of blessed memory), Jonathan Omer-Man, Susie Schneider, David Wolfe-Blank (of blessed memory), and David Zeller (of blessed memory). I thank them for the wisdom they have passed on to me.

My greatest learning as a teacher has taken place at Chochmat HaLev, a center of Jewish meditation in the San Francisco Bay area. I wish to thank my students there for teaching me so much through their questions, observations, and experiences.

I appreciate the careful reading of this manuscript by Marcia Freedman and Sandy Butler, and I thank Sandy Boucher for the thought-provoking discussions about Buddhism and Judaism. I also thank Peter Levitt, Shirley Graham, Deena Metzger, and Michael Hill for our stimulating conversations about mystical experience. The presence of the women in my women's group, the Wandering Menstruals, helped to nourish me during the writing process.

I am grateful for the lessons I have learned from my mother, Vera (of blessed memory), and my children, Michelle, Lisa, and Nick, and their partners. My grandchildren, Sarah, Jackie, Nathan, Elias, and Jack, provide me with amazing insights, and I thank them.

My deepest appreciation goes to my husband and spiritual partner, Jonathan. His loving support during these months helped to give me the strength and courage to write this book. In his wisdom, he knew when to make suggestions and when to remain silent. To him, then, I most gratefully dedicate this book.

PART ONE

The Practice of Jewish Meditation

1
What Is Jewish Meditation?

Over the years you've undoubtedly had experiences that were spiritual in nature. Perhaps they took place while you were reading a poem, or holding a sleeping child. Or walking in the woods, or watching the sunset. Or while you were praying.

These experiences—and more—have helped you know that something exists beyond your regular, everyday reality. This "something" is what I call "the silence within." To many of us this state seems both familiar and mysterious. It has the quality of spaciousness, and it appears to have no boundaries.

Like a pregnant pause, the silence within contains all possibility. It is the raw material of creation, the formlessness that exists before the concrete emerges. When we enter into this state, we have our most intense spiritual experiences and receive our most significant moments of understanding.

If you are like many people, you probably don't pay much attention to the silence within as you rush from place to place, juggling responsibilities and meeting deadlines. But you sense its existence. In the quiet moments it hovers just outside your consciousness, and you are drawn to it. It might even frighten you, the scary unknown.

The world's major religious traditions acknowledge the existence of the silence within. Whatever name they give it, or however they describe it, they see it as something that can be explored. Each tradition has created ways for doing this, and passes them on to succeeding generations.

Likewise, nontraditional spiritual teachers, such as those in the New Age movement, assume that transcendence of everyday life can take place. The experience of the spiritual realm, they say, does not depend on a traditional belief in God or adherence to a particular religion.

In these times of spiritual seeking, many people are turning to Jewish meditation as a pathway to the silence within. They are discovering that the practice is wise and beautiful, and that over the years it can lead to great spiritual transformation.

In the pages ahead, you will be introduced to Jewish meditation. You will learn about its background, as well as its techniques. This will enable you to use it creatively in your life. When you understand it in its fullness, you will see its enormous strength. And when you learn how to practice it, you will receive the great gift of its living presence in the years ahead.

What Is Jewish Meditation?

Most simply, Jewish meditation is a spiritual practice found within the Jewish tradition.

The best way to describe it is to consider its name. The word "Jewish" is included because meditation has been—and is—a part of Judaism. Traditionally it exists alongside other aspects of Jewish observance, such as prayer and Torah study. Less traditionally, it is done alone as a spiritual practice.

Jewish meditation uses images, words, and symbols that come from the Jewish tradition. The meditations themselves, and the teachings that go along with them, reflect Jewish understanding. Because of this, people who are introduced to Jewish meditation will not mistake it for any other meditative practice.

Now we move on to the "meditation" word in Jewish meditation. Meditation is a specific kind of activity that involves directing the mind. It follows a prescribed order, and it uses techniques different from ordinary thinking or daydreaming. The activity takes place during a prescribed time period, and thereby has a beginning and an end. Although the contents of Jewish meditation are unique in many ways, it joins other meditative traditions in directing the mind to the silence within.

Jewish meditation can be further described as an organic practice that has grown and changed through history. Although it is part of Judaism, it nevertheless has absorbed elements from other traditions, such as Sufism, Gnosticism, and Buddhism. The practice contains a great variety of teachings and meditations. At different times creative bursts of collective insight into the use of meditation have taken place. One, in fact, is going on right now.

How Does Jewish Meditation Compare to Other Kinds of Meditation?

Jewish meditation aims toward exploring the silence within. In this way it is like other religious meditative traditions. All of them direct meditators to let go of their everyday concerns and ordinary patterns of thinking as they open their minds to spiritual experience.

Most religious traditions consider meditation to be an important path to personal transformation. So too does

Judaism. One of the ways this takes place is through self-refinement. During meditation, our ego defenses dissolve and we become more aware of who we really are. We then can act to strengthen our positive qualities and diminish or transform those qualities that are destructive. As a result, we are able to make more of a contribution to those around us and to the world. Our inner "light" or "soul" becomes more revealed.

A further similarity between Jewish meditation and most other traditions is found in the intention to bring the meditator closer to God. In past centuries this was *the* reason for Jews to meditate. The meditator yearned to close the distance between the self and the Divine, and meditation was the vehicle for this to take place. Today, the emphasis on connecting to the Divine still exists, although we teach and practice meditation in ways that are not necessarily the same as those of past centuries.

Jewish meditation resembles other religious meditative traditions also in that it holds the understanding that we have a responsibility to make the world a better place. Buddhists regularly perform acts of service, and Christians are guided by the edict to "love your neighbor as yourself." Jews commit themselves to *tikkun olam* (repairing and healing the world). Meditation alone is not enough: We also must become involved in changing the world. This basic tenet of Judaism is fulfilled even more effectively when we retreat into meditation for periods of time. Within meditation, we can find the strength, the balance, and the purpose we need to continue this task.

We've discussed some of the similarities between Jewish meditation and other religious traditions. But what about relaxation meditation, that popular antidote for illness and emotional distress? There are similarities here too. Both use specific techniques to enter into a state of meditation. These techniques sometimes appear to be the same, as in meditations that focus on the breath.

The point of this type of meditation is to relax so that restoration and healing can take place. But we can't relax if our minds are whirling around. Likewise, we can't enter into the silence within if our minds are spinning out of control. We must find a way to stop the busyness. Meditation provides this, whether the end goal is to relax or to transcend our ordinary reality.

All forms of meditation—including Jewish meditation—share a common base of techniques. But differences exist in their purposes and how they are used. In transcendental meditation, the meditator repeats a mantra again and again. The mind focuses on the sound, although it has no inherent meaning to most meditators. In Jewish meditation, the same mantra technique is sometimes used, but meditators are instructed to focus on Hebrew letters or words. The goal is for them to become "filled" with these letters or words, and to merge with them so that they enter into a deep meditative state and experience the presence of the Divine. An example is the *Sh'ma* meditation, which you will find in chapter 6. This meditation is based on the traditional *Sh'ma,* a prayer that proclaims the unity of the Divine. The words of this prayer are repeated silently, like a mantra, and the meditator is instructed to pay attention to their sound, not to their meaning. Even so, these words are undeniably Jewish and they resonate with most Jews.

The most obvious way in which Jewish meditation differs from other traditions is its Jewish context. Jewish meditation is part of Judaism, not Sufism, Buddhism, or any other religion. It developed through the centuries as a Jewish pathway to the Holy, and it was practiced by those committed to traditional religious Judaism.

Today, many Jews are adopting Jewish meditation as a spiritual practice without taking on rigorous Jewish observance. They are discovering that it gives their lives spiritual meaning. Still, Jewish meditation is so strongly grounded in

Judaism that they experience it as Jewish meditation rather than general meditation.

Jewish meditation can be distinguished from other meditative traditions also by its content. The meditations come from the wellspring of Jewish understanding, and they include Jewish symbols, words, and images. Although some of them have themes found in other traditions—such as the *chesed* (loving-kindness) meditation in this book—they also are located within Judaism.

But perhaps the most important difference between Jewish meditation and other traditions is how it feels to sit in a room with others who are doing this practice. The experience is not like Buddhist or Hindu or Sufi meditation. For many of us, it feels like coming home.

What Is the Relationship between Jewish Meditation, Jewish Mysticism, and Kabbalah?

Jewish meditation is a technique rooted in certain understandings. The main philosophical base of Jewish meditation is Jewish mysticism. This tradition has existed throughout Jewish history, and it centers on an intimate, immediate contact with the Divine. Many of the images we use for meditation and the ideas we teach come from it.

Jewish mysticism seeks to answer the basic questions of life, such as the nature of God, the meaning of creation, and the existence of good and evil. It transmits understanding through the study of mystical texts like the *Sefer Yetzirah,* which was written between the third and sixth centuries C.E., and the *Zohar,* which was written toward the end of the thirteenth century. The language of mysticism is poetic and evocative, and it opens the imagination to perceiving God in new ways.

Jewish mysticism has an experiential side. It considers meditation to be a pathway to an intense connection with the Divine. Through the centuries mystics have taught their students the meditations they've devised, and some of them have been written down. Jewish meditation, as we know it today, draws meditations from this great treasury, as well as from other sources.

It is important to understand that Jewish mysticism has always had strong ties to traditional Judaism. The mystics of the past had rigorous Jewish practices, even though they saw the Holy Cosmos in nontraditional ways. Their spiritual experience through meditation added depth to their religious commitment rather than providing an alternative way of life.

If Jewish mysticism is the base of Jewish meditation, what about Kabbalah? This word, which is bandied around a lot these days, often confuses beginning meditators.

Kabbalah means "to receive" in Hebrew. It refers to the mystical tradition within Judaism from the twelfth century to the present day. Like the rest of Jewish mysticism, it is directed to the experience of union with the Divine.

The Kabbalah can be described as a nontraditional response to spiritual concerns. God, for instance, is seen as indwelling as well as transcendent, and as both male and female. The world is perceived as ever-changing, radiant, and reflective of the Divine. All life contains sparks of holiness. These understandings differ from the traditional view of God as outside the natural world and separate from humankind.

The Jewish mystical tradition, including the Kabbalah, is a collection of many teachings about the structure and nature of reality. It has evolved through the centuries. We speak of it as though it is a completed point of view, but it is like a tree sending out new branches in surprising directions: Its shape is still emerging.

What Are the Historical Roots of Jewish Meditation?

Jewish meditation goes back a long way. Some scholars suggest that it was indicated even in the Torah, the first five books of the Bible. They note that Isaac engaged in an activity that appears to be meditative: "And Isaac went out to walk in the field in the evening" (Genesis 24:63). According to some interpretations, this experience of meditation or prayer was so intense that his presence radiated outward, causing Rebecca, his bride-to-be, to fall off her camel when she first saw him. Jacob too seems to have entered a meditative state when he isolated himself in preparation for his reunion with his brother Esau: "Jacob was left alone" (Genesis 32:25). In his solitude he wrestled with an angel—just as we sometimes struggle with our desires and fears during meditation.

Other hints of the existence of meditation can be found in the Psalms. These prayers describe the yearning that leads to the spiritual experience that we most often associate with meditation or prayer: "My soul yearns for You, my flesh pines for You" (Psalm 63:2). They also show us the importance of becoming connected to the Divine: "I have continuously placed God before me; God is at my right hand so that I shall not falter" (Psalm 16:8).

At the time the Bible was completed, around 400 B.C.E., meditation appears to have been widespread. A few sources claim that over a million Israelites meditated on a regular basis, although most say that this figure is wildly exaggerated.

Meditation during this post-Biblical period—and for many centuries thereafter—can be described as apocalyptic and visionary. People learned to focus their minds on fiery chariots, angelic hosts, wild beasts, and sometimes-terrifying images of Divine majesty. Accounts of these meditations sound hallucinatory to our contemporary ears.

When the Jews were dispersed into other countries after the fall of the Second Temple in 70 C.E., many of them continued to meditate. Rabbis spoke out against this practice, however, because they feared that it would lead to abandonment of Judaism. Meditators might be tempted to try out foreign spiritual practices, and eventually they would be seduced away from the tradition of their birth.

Over time, Jewish meditation seems to have gone underground. By the Middle Ages, only small, select groups of religious men continued the practice. Most people weren't even introduced to it: The prescription held that one must be male, over forty, and married to study Kabbalah and to meditate. This elitist control over meditation remained in effect for many centuries until the Hasidic movement began in Eastern Europe in the eighteenth century.

In the meanwhile, Jewish mysticism and Jewish meditation continued to develop through the writing and teaching of the Kabbalists. For example, Abraham Abulafia in the thirteenth century devised meditations that focused on the name of God and the pure forms of the letters of the Hebrew alphabet, and Isaac Luria in the sixteenth century transmitted a radical mystical understanding of creation that was the basis of many meditations. The insights of great teachers such as these helped to shape Jewish mysticism and meditation as we know it today.

During the centuries before the Hasidic movement, Jewish meditation consisted mainly of focusing on the letters of the Divine Name in various combinations—a practice thought to be dangerous for the uninitiated. Once Hasidism became established in Eastern Europe, however, meditation became more accessible. Rabbis in the eighteenth and nineteenth centuries brought it into widespread use by teaching that prayer could be done as a mantra. Anyone could climb the spiritual ladder through all the states of being and experience the opening of the heavens by praying in this meditative way. These rabbis also developed contemplative forms of meditation aimed at helping people increase their awareness of God's presence and refine their character traits.

In its heyday Hasidism had hundreds of thousands of adherents. But by the twentieth century it had shrunk in size and influence, and meditation was less a part of religious practice. Many Hasidic rabbis who knew how to do it died during the Holocaust.

Until recently, the existence of Jewish meditation was barely known in the United States. Mainstream American Jews historically have viewed spirituality with suspicion. As a result, synagogues and Jewish organizations have failed to support the spiritual quest, and seekers have had to look outside their own tradition to learn a meditative practice.

But this is changing. In the last three decades, the word about Jewish meditation has gotten out. Aryeh Kaplan, an Orthodox rabbi, wrote several books on the subject in the 1970s and 1980s. Other publications followed that helped to break through the wall of ignorance. Meditative texts from past centuries are now being translated and taught. Several centers of Jewish meditation exist in the United States, and undoubtedly more will be established. Meditation classes and sitting groups are proliferating, synagogues are bringing the practice into their communities, and several conferences on the practice have been convened.

As more people experience Jewish meditation's power and wisdom, they are helping to spread it further within the Jewish world. After centuries of being hidden, meditation finally is beginning to be accepted as a legitimate part of American Judaism.

What Is Jewish Meditation Like Today?

Jewish meditation is a stream fed by three sources.

The first is the Jewish meditative tradition. Some of the meditations we teach come from past centuries, discovered within old texts or passed down orally from teacher to student.

The second source of Jewish meditation is the creative work of meditation teachers today. Using Jewish symbols and images, we are fashioning meditations that are especially meaningful for people in this postmodern era. Although these meditations are "new," in the sense that we have no record of them being done before, they build respectfully on the contributions of teachers in the past and on the tradition of Jewish meditation.

Jewish meditation is being influenced by a third source: Buddhism. In recent decades many Jews have adopted Buddhist meditative practices. Almost a third of American Buddhists are Jewish by birth. Many of these people have found a spiritual path within Buddhism that they didn't find within Judaism, but they want to reconnect with their Jewish roots. We are pleased to introduce them to Jewish meditation. As they learn about it, they bring the knowledge and wisdom gained from Buddhism to their practices. Their insights help to shape the direction of Jewish meditation.

If you look at current teachers of Jewish meditation, you will see that we don't all teach the same material or use the same approach. This is because we come from different backgrounds. Some of us, as traditionalists, are committed to passing on meditations learned from Kabbalistic or Hasidic sources. Others blend these traditional meditations with contemporary ones. Many bring Zen or Vipassana insight meditation into the Jewish setting, and they teach Buddhist awareness practice along with other, more traditional Jewish meditations.

The differences continue: Some teachers think that Jewish meditation includes meditative singing, chanting, and movement. Others hold to a more strict definition, saying that the practice should be done by sitting and focusing in a traditional way. They consider these more expressive techniques to be meditative warm-ups, and dismiss them as not the real thing.

The different approaches have not been integrated, although efforts are being made in that direction. Meditation teachers, for instance, are discussing how to bring in elements of Buddhist practice without losing Jewish meditation's essential character. In time, there will be more clarity—although I wager there will always be various schools of thought about the nature and practice of Jewish meditation.

The variety in teaching styles resulting from this lack of agreement can confuse beginning meditators. They often ask, "What is proper Jewish meditation, anyhow?" The answer is that no one way is "best" or "more Jewish." Each has something to offer.

In this discussion about Jewish meditation today we haven't yet mentioned a most obvious and important fact: The practice is now open to everyone. Thankfully, you no longer have to be male or traditionally observant or Jewish to practice Jewish meditation.

The effects of this change are already apparent. People from all backgrounds feel welcomed into Jewish meditation. And as they become involved, they bring their unique perspectives and insights to the practice. They are part of the creative process, helping to develop a meditative practice that includes but extends beyond traditional concerns. Through sharing their experience, they are contributing to the shape of Jewish meditation for the future.

Let us take a few minutes to focus on the breath.

The breath is central in Jewish meditation. It connects us to the rhythms of the universe and helps us quiet our minds.

We will stop at the end of these first few chapters to pay attention to the breath. This will help you become mindful of its qualities and integrate moments of meditation into your study of Jewish meditation. It also will teach you how to begin the core meditations in part two.

Now, inhale deeply. Let your breath fill you.

As you exhale, make a sound. Any sound. It can be a sigh or a shout or a musical note—whatever feels right to you in this moment. Don't analyze it or attribute meaning to it. Just let it be.

Draw the sound out as long as you can.

When your lungs have deflated, let them become filled once again. As you exhale this breath, make another sound.

Do this several times: the breath in, the breath out with sound.

When you are finished, sit quietly for a few moments.

2
The Promise of Jewish Meditation

If you are like most people, you have tried to improve yourself throughout your life. In our culture we value this pursuit, as can be seen by the shelves of psychology books in bookstores, the proliferation of self-help groups, and the popularity of psychotherapy. But despite your efforts to change, you probably sense that you are not yet the person you are meant to be.

Jewish mysticism addresses this concern. It posits that each of us is a unique being, or soul, and that we have certain tasks to accomplish during our lifetimes. These tasks are specific: Yours might be to learn to let go of your anger and open your heart, while mine is to transform my unruly pride into humility.

Usually we don't have any idea what our tasks are until we've lived for a while. But certain experiences—the same feeling of envy popping up again and again, the same nagging unhappiness, the same failure of relationships—help us identify our patterns. Our central issues become clearer. We no longer can blame others for all that goes wrong, and we start to take responsibility for our actions.

Now we are ready to commit ourselves to the task of spiritually healing those negative, broken places within ourselves. In Jewish mysticism this is considered "self-refinement." The point of it is not to feel better—although that can happen—but to transform ourselves so that we become more effective in our lives and participate in *tikkun olam,* repairing the world.

The connection between healing the self and healing the world takes place on two levels. On the everyday level we are able to contribute more to those around us as we do this work. We develop the capacity to give with an open and loving heart, and our presence radiates outward, having effects on others that we do not know. On the mystical level our souls are in need of healing as much as anything else. As our destructive qualities begin to dissolve and our souls move to a higher plane and become more connected to the Source of All Being, they are part of the healing of the world, *tikkun olam.*

Self-refinement never stops. Because we are human, we remain in a state of incompletion. Living in our bodies, investing in relationships, striving to survive, we never fully transcend our brokenness. We are caught in our own warring impulses and desires. Although we are able to become increasingly connected to the Holy, there's always more work to do.

Jewish meditation is a vehicle for profound personal and spiritual change. Along with prayer, it is where we do self-refinement. It helps to transform us so that we become more spiritually receptive. It gives us understanding so that we act differently in the world. Rather than strike out at a family member who irritates us, for instance, we now respond more compassionately. Our hours and our days become fruitful in ways we never expected.

How Does Jewish Meditation Bring About Personal Change?

Jewish meditation changes us, but it does not produce immediate results. As with any other spiritual practice, it may take months, years, decades.

I know people who start to meditate, then drop it within a short time because they don't see a difference in their lives. This attitude is not surprising in our quick-fix culture. A more realistic approach is to meditate without looking for instant improvement. If you put aside your analytical self-consciousness, the differences that come from meditation will make themselves known in their own subtle ways. You then will have the pleasure of discovering them, rather than subjecting yourself to preconceived notions of transformation.

Still, I respect the desire of beginning meditators to learn about the possibilities of change. Most of us decide to meditate because we think something will come from it. Otherwise, why spend ten or twenty minutes sitting silently when we could be doing something else?

One of the ways Jewish meditation brings about change is by teaching *concentration*. Ordinarily our thoughts jump from subject to subject, but during meditation the mind is directed to stay on course. As you learn to channel your thoughts, you will be able to focus more intently on one thing at a time. Then you will experience it in a fuller way.

In meditation your experience of the spiritual realm will deepen as you learn to concentrate. If you focus meditatively for twenty minutes on the letters of the name of God, for example, your mind will be drawn in a spiritual direction at least part of that time. Chances are that you wouldn't enter this same mind-state during the same twenty minutes without the help of meditation: You'd more likely be worrying, or planning, or filling your mind in countless other ways.

In your everyday life the ability to concentrate can help you think more clearly and stay mentally on track. A certain sharpness develops over time, an ability to be single-minded that is important in the creative process.

Another change that comes with Jewish meditation is increased *awareness*. During meditation we observe our thoughts and watch them rise and fall away. We learn what they are, and we find out how our minds work. Our obsessions, passions, fears, and mental quirks come to the surface. Although this might sound disturbing, most people experience it as a great relief. They've sensed these things within themselves all along, and they finally discover that they are not so terrible after all.

Increased awareness during meditation leads to greater knowledge of the self. This understanding is important in the self-refinement I described above. Taking the time to explore the broken places within ourselves can lead to great healing. I am not talking here about endless self-analysis, but about noticing those places within that are unbalanced.

A more developed awareness also can be useful in everyday life. If you pay attention to what you think and feel, you are more likely to be present in your relationships and in your work. You can negotiate the difficulties that arise with greater honesty and kindness.

Meditation helps us become less attached to our thoughts. We see them come and go, and we realize that they are not permanent. Ultimately, they are unimportant. And so are we. This is a hard lesson for most of us because we like to think of ourselves as the center of the universe. But once we accept that we aren't, we can experience ourselves as part of the unfolding of life. This opens us up to deeper spiritual understanding.

Meditators often report that they experience the spiritual dimension of life in a heightened way after they've been meditating for a while. They are more aware of the shimmering leaves on the trees, the crisp sound of water, and the dank smell of earth. Not only do they see beauty, but all of life is more vivid, more "real." They more accurately read the expressions on people's faces and feel the pain in the world.

A final way in which Jewish meditation brings about transformation is by *heightening spiritual experience.* As we have more connection, more contact with the Divine—in whatever way that is experienced—we cannot help but be affected. Some people report that they've found a place of inner security that had been missing before. Others say that they finally have a sense of meaning after a lifetime of alienation. Whatever the outcome, it cannot help but shift our perception of the world.

How Will Jewish Meditation Affect Your Connection with Judaism?

All of the changes I've described above probably sound appealing. Who among us doesn't want to become more focused, more aware, more spiritually attuned and closer to the Divine? But you might be wondering what this has to do with being Jewish.

Many Jewish meditators are completely secular when they begin to practice. They may have investigated other meditative traditions in their search for spiritual meaning. However, they still yearn to be connected to the tradition of Judaism. Jewish meditation offers them this possibility.

Secular people can enter Jewish meditation without feeling that they are violating their values. The practice does not require a belief in the traditional patriarchal God, nor membership in a synagogue or temple. Meditators' experience with other traditions only adds to their ability to do Jewish meditation, because certain meditation skills are transferable.

Once they've started a practice, they often become enormously interested in Judaism. I've known many such meditators who end up committed to the Jewish path—much to their surprise. However, they still value and retain what they've learned elsewhere, and bring it into their renewed Jewish lives.

Sometimes it takes a period of time for people to feel comfortable exploring the roots of Jewish meditation. They need to get beyond their ambivalence about Judaism as a religion. Many still are angry about being forced as children to go to Hebrew school or sit through boring services. Others are upset that Judaism historically is a patriarchy. Once they begin to see that this inequality is changing in dramatic and significant ways, they discover that they can relate to the tradition. They take from it the parts that are meaningful and discard those that are unacceptable.

Jews who are already religious also are drawn to Jewish meditation. When they realize that it has been a part of Jewish tradition for centuries, they accept it as legitimate. They would not explore Buddhist meditation, but they are open to learning Jewish meditation since it is grounded in their own tradition. They usually are pleased to discover that it supplements their already established Jewish religious practice. Many report that their prayer life deepens as they integrate meditation into it.

Jewish meditation appeals to many non-Jews. For those interested in learning about Judaism or exploring conversion, meditation is a good entry point. The practice contains universal attributes found in other meditative traditions, thus making it appear accessible, even familiar.

People from all kinds of backgrounds practice Jewish meditation. They do it together, without the usual problems of religious Jew versus secular person, or learned Jew versus neophyte. Jewish meditation is an equalizer within the Jewish world: The familiar divisions between people disappear. Anyone can practice it, and no special group claims it as its own.

Will Jewish meditation bring you closer to Judaism? Probably. But this will come about because you desire it, not because it is imposed upon you.

What Is the Value of a Meditation Practice?

If you are at an event or a Jewish service and you are led in meditation, you probably appreciate the experience. It might even be a significant moment in your life. This experience is not a practice, however. A practice of meditation means that you are committed to meditation, and you do it regularly.

A difference exists, however, between enjoying meditation when it happens to be offered or when you think of it, and taking it on as your own spiritual practice. This difference can be likened to that between dating and a committed relationship. When you date someone your level of involvement is low. If the date goes well and you enjoy yourself, you'll probably arrange another; further contact depends on the success of each encounter. But in a committed relationship there will be times of struggle and distance. There also will be times of the deepest connectedness. The commitment remains no matter what, and it supersedes all the fluctuations of mood and circumstance. So it is with a meditation practice.

Recently, a beginning student asked if it is acceptable to meditate only at difficult times. He spoke about his anxiety in his present job and his hope that meditation would help to dissipate it. He wanted to use meditation to relieve his discomfort whenever it arose. Certainly this student can do as he likes. But if he were to meditate regularly, he would gain far more from it. His skill would increase as he becomes familiar with the process and with himself as a meditator.

Meditation is like a muscle that needs to be developed. Its strength depends on regular exercise. If we call upon it only at certain difficult moments or whenever we're in the mood, it possibly will serve us. But not as well as if we nourish it and maintain it.

This book is a guide to setting up a Jewish meditation practice. Some of you will be ready to take this step. Others won't. Or you'll consider it, try it out, meditate for a while, drop it, and do it again—until you finally settle into committing yourself.

Then you will discover the richness of a meditation practice. You'll find out that you have the capacity to commit yourself and to stay with that commitment. Even those times when you are bored or restless or frustrated will become part of the growing experience. You will learn that the effort is worth it, because at the oddest moment, the most surprising time, you'll have experiences beyond your imagination.

What about God in Meditation?

The subject of God raises more questions and discussion than any other subject among the students in my meditation classes. I always devote a chunk of time to it because if I don't, students' concerns will remain a stumbling block to meditation. Besides, I always learn something from the process.

Everybody has an idea about the nature of God. What is yours? Before we continue, take a few minutes and let your words or images about God come to your mind. Write them down if you can.

Some of you undoubtedly will respond to this short exercise by exclaiming that you don't believe in God. But think about it a little more carefully: Belief in God is an abstract notion. We "objectively" view the evidence for God's existence, then we decide if it stacks up to our preconceived notions of what the Divine must be. If it does, we say we believe in God. If it doesn't, we consider ourselves to be atheists or agnostics.

I've found it far more helpful to use experience as a guide. Rather than searching for a God that we've already decided has certain characteristics, or trying to disprove the existence of this God, we need to be open to other possibilities.

People often experience the presence of the Holy, but not in the ways they were led to think were "God." They fail to acknowledge the many facets of their spiritual awareness. Or they are so wrapped up in their daily lives that they don't let in much of the spiritual presence, or "God," that is always there.

No two understandings of God are the same. Everyone stumbles when faced with the task of defining the Divine. It's like blindfolded people trying to determine the main element of a wood-framed window while touching only a small part. One person says it's glass, while another swears it's wood.

The Jewish tradition recognizes that it is impossible to put the essence of God into words. In fact, it opposes the idea of even trying. God is the Ineffable, the Mystery, the One Who Transcends All Labels. The true name of the Divine is never uttered; it is beyond human knowledge. Therefore, Judaism has many Hebrew names for God, representing different aspects of Divine Being. Among the most familiar are *Adonai, Elohim, El, Shekhinah, Yah,* and *Melekh.*

This subtlety about the nature of God is not as apparent in the Torah, however. The Divine is presented there in a most patriarchal way: God grants favors when He is pleased and punishes when He is angered. He—always male and always capitalized—is compassionate toward the Israelites at times, but also vengeful, moody, and chauvinistic. He wipes out people seemingly on a whim. This God is at the heart of patriarchal Judaism.

Many of us consider the Torah portrayal of God as inadequate or even offensive. We experience the Divine differently. As my seven-year-old granddaughter says, "When I was little, I used to think that God was a man high up in the sky, but now I think that God is mixed into everything and is between everything—like the dolphins and the sea."

The Kabbalistic mystics had an understanding of God that was much broader than the Torah image. The Divine is seen as indwelling as well as transcendent, and as feminine as well as masculine. The sparks of God are present in all life so that nothing is devoid of holiness. God is dynamic rather than static: Creation continues in every moment, and all life participates with God.

I don't mean to say that the mystics of earlier centuries had perfect understanding. Even though they saw God as both male and female, they upheld traditional gender roles in their daily lives. But the poetry of the Kabbalah, and its imagination, express a vision of God that today many of us still find meaningful. This vision goes beyond simple explanation to intimations of possibility that circle beyond the reaches of our minds.

In the end, most of us find our way toward the Holy Presence in life, whether we call it God or not. Through meditation we open ourselves up to spiritual experience and to the silence within.

Often, students who are unsure about God's existence ask me if I think they can start practicing Jewish meditation. Of course they can. We are all seekers, after all.

What Must You Know to Begin Jewish Meditation?

I've discovered that students sometimes are intimidated by the Jewish context of Jewish meditation. Although they are competent in many other areas, they feel insecure because they never had a Jewish education or they never learned the Hebrew language.

Judaism is seen by many people as being intellectually demanding. We are the People of the Book, and our tradition emphasizes learning. Talmud and Torah study, which consist of intellectual wrangling as well as text elucidation, are holy activities, and those adept at them are revered in the Orthodox world.

It's true that the life of the mind is highly valued in Judaism, but don't let that deter you from beginning to meditate. Jewish meditation is not about being smart; it's about opening yourself up spiritually.

In fact, everyone is on equal footing in Jewish meditation. A scholar in Jewish history is not necessarily a more adept meditator than someone who is ignorant about the fall of the Second Temple. I've found that people who don't know much about Judaism settle quickly into meditation once they get beyond their initial insecurity, because they are not burdened with as many internal negative messages, such as "Jews shouldn't meditate" or "Meditation is dangerous."

Once they begin, they often become excited about Judaism and want to learn more. Soon they're studying Hebrew and taking classes in Jewish history and Jewish liturgy. Meditation provides an entrance for them into Judaism.

Let us return to the breath.

Make yourself comfortable by adjusting your sitting position. If you are cramped or constricted, you will not be able to breathe deeply.

Now, draw in your breath. Feel your
chest and abdomen expand.

Let out your breath with a sound, as
you did before. Any sound. A
gentle sigh or a shout, a moan or
a whoop.

Feel the sound reverberate through
you,
Releasing tension,
Expressing the inexpressible.
Let the sound be what it is.

Do this several times, then return to
your normal breathing.

Feel yourself begin to relax.
The breath in. The breath out. An easy
flow. Neither too much nor too
little. Just the right amount to
sustain you.
Simply watch your breath.
Its rise. Its fall.

Continue in this way for a few minutes, then return to the book.

3

States of Consciousness

If you have never meditated before, you probably wonder what the experience will be like. Perhaps you've heard accounts of meditators slipping into states of rapture or despair. These images, popular in our culture, are enough to concern anyone who cares about continuing in an everyday life routine.

People who meditate know that the reality of the practice is far more mundane. We sit and we sit, and nothing significant seems to be happening. Still, over time we enter into many different mind-states, or states of consciousness. These are not unique to meditation, as they can be reached in other ways, such as through prayer. But a meditation practice provides the opportunity for us to experience them intensely.

During meditation we are more aware of what we are thinking and feeling because we choose to spend this time focusing on our internal mental processes rather than busying ourselves with other activities. Meditation clears away a lot of the static in our minds so that we can see what's there. Often it's no surprise; other times it astonishes us beyond belief.

Language is inadequate when it comes to describing various states of consciousness reached during meditation. An experience that is profound and complex becomes flat when summarized. Its subtleties are lost, and it appears different than it was.

Yet new students always want to hear about the possibilities of consciousness. Even though I explain that every meditator is different, they say that they feel more secure if they know what others before them have experienced.

This chapter is an attempt to provide you with some previews of where meditation might take you. But remember that meditative experience does not fit neatly into words, and that you should not expect to have the same experience as anyone else.

Each of us is on a spiritual journey—a unique spiritual journey. We need to discover what emerges along our path. If we try to manufacture our experiences to fit into preconceived categories, we will fail. All we can do is begin to meditate and see where it takes us. Once we let go of trying to control the process, we will recognize the gifts that are there for us.

What Does the Jewish Mystical Tradition Say about Mind-States During Meditation?

Teachers of Jewish meditation in past centuries were not interested in describing the full panoply of consciousness. For the most part, their greatest concern was to draw closer to God. They described the feelings that preceded this state—the deep yearning and the burning desire for connection. But the actual experience of attachment to the Divine, or *devekut*, as it is called, is not categorized and analyzed intellectually in

Jewish writings. This shouldn't surprise us, as anything to do with God is by its very nature beyond words.

We find powerful poetic expressions of *devekut* in the Bible, however. The Psalms are filled with descriptions of the heartache and yearning for contact with the Divine, and the experience of connectedness: "Adonai, hear my prayer, and let my cry come to You. Hide not Your face from me" (Psalm 102:2–3). "Where could I go from Your spirit, or where could I flee from Your Presence? If I would ascend to heaven, You are there; and if I were to make my bed in the grave, You are there. If I were to take the wings of the dawn and dwell in the uttermost part of the sea, even there Your hand would lead me, and Your right hand would hold me" (Psalm 139:7–10).

The concept of *devekut* has remained important in Jewish meditation. The word is usually translated as "cleaving" or "attachment" to the Divine. I think of it like an infant wrapped in its mother's arms: All the barriers are down, and though the mother and child are two separate beings, they are as one.

The tradition understands that this holy state is transitory. We sometimes experience it, but it evaporates quickly for most of us. Inevitably we return to everyday consciousness. As embodied beings with complicated lives, we cannot do otherwise. Still, traces of the experience remain. In very diluted form, the memory of it stays with us and informs our perceptions and our actions.

The desire to reach the state of *devekut* is strong, but how do we get there? In Judaism we find the concept of *kavvanah,* translated as "holy intention." This refers to being in a ready, directed state when we meditate or pray. The tradition understands that a relationship exists between the intention of the seeker and the spiritual experience that follows. We're like the archer who sights the target while drawing back the bow: If we aim carefully in the right direction, we're more likely to reach the target.

In Jewish meditation we recognize the importance of *kavvanah* and strive to meditate with a pure intention, one that is not clouded by ulterior motives such as impressing other people or proving something to ourselves. We have to diminish our ego involvement in our performance as meditators before our *kavvanah* can be strong and move us toward *devekut.*

Another useful idea about meditative consciousness within Jewish mysticism is *hitbodedut.* This refers to the act of drawing into the self, or self-isolation. The tradition recognizes that our everyday environment assaults us with information and demands. Therefore, we are encouraged to spend time in nature or sequester ourselves in a private space to meditate. We cannot enter the silence within if the outside noise is too great. Rabbi Nachman, a great early nineteenth-century Hasidic teacher, even recommended pulling the sheet over our heads at night to meditate if that is the only way we can experience *hitbodedut.*

The understanding of *hitbodedut* is expanded within Jewish mysticism to include emotional and psychic distance from our daily lives. As we meditate we sometimes find ourselves moving into a state of consciousness beyond our ordinary thoughts and concerns. This internal isolation doesn't happen automatically: We have to develop the ability to distance ourselves from our familiar mental preoccupations.

Jewish mysticism goes even further by saying that through meditation we isolate our soul, or essence, from the rest of our being. As our internal mental chatter quiets down, we move into greater spiritual realms. We exist in those moments as soul rather than as self. Our awareness of daily concerns and our ego distractions are not present. This state of internal isolation is also called *hitbodedut.*

A final state of consciousness described in the mystical tradition is *teshuvah,* translated as "return." You might have heard this word used during the High Holy Days when we talk about making amends for our misdeeds of the past year, setting our lives straight, and returning to God.

Through meditation we sometimes experience ourselves as part of the Divine Whole. We no longer are single beings: The all-important "I" has temporarily disappeared. At these times we are in a state of *teshuvah,* or return to our essential nature. We are one with God. Boundaries do not exist. We feel that we are in a place we left long ago, like Adam or Eve returning to the Garden of Eden. In this state of consciousness we experience great healing.

Like other mind-states, *teshuvah* does not last. But we are deeply affected by this experience of our holiness and the holiness of all life. We see our everyday routines through a different lens, one that is more God-centered. Concerns that we thought were monumental are now experienced as part of the great cosmos.

What Other Experiences Are Common during Meditation?

The Jewish mystical tradition gives us an indication of some of the most profound states of mind possible through meditation. Others exist, however.

Many meditators say that they've had the experience of their hearts opening during meditation: Anger slips away, and they are filled with a deep love for all life. In this state they experience themselves as a channel, receiving love from the Divine, passing it along to others. This love is not foolish or misinformed: It acknowledges human frailty. But it goes beyond the critical faculty to an appreciation of the beauty and holiness that is in every being.

Many people also talk about feeling "lighter" during and after meditation. As they let go of their ordinary concerns, they experience great joy. Life's difficulties haven't disappeared, but they no longer seem to be such an impossible burden.

Sometimes students ask if they should be having visions during meditation. They point to descriptions of this experience in literature, including the Bible. But I answer that most people don't have visions. And when they do, we consider them to be just another mental fabrication, not a pipeline to the truth of the universe. They might be interesting, but they do not indicate that the meditator has reached a higher consciousness.

Fear is another mind-state that meditators experience at times. It can surface unexpectedly, and when it does, our breathing becomes shallow, our hearts race, and we feel alarmed. Fear, however, is only a response to a set of thoughts or a disturbing body sensation. Students find that it quickly fades away once they observe it and name it. But if they become anxious or worry that their fear will hurt them, the experience can be prolonged. This is an important lesson, especially for students who have led fearful lives. Through meditation they finally are able to deal with ordinary moments of fear without panicking.

Fear is not the only difficult state that meditators may experience. Most of us resist sitting still without distraction, so we become agitated or restless or bored. The minutes drag by, and we hardly know what to do with ourselves. Our minds jump around from subject to subject, refusing to stay with the meditation. Or we become so sleepy that we can hardly keep track of what we are doing.

We also get sidetracked by our physical complaints. The sore knee or the back pain that we ordinarily ignore suddenly flares up and captures all our attention. How can we possibly sit still when our bodies hurt so much? We begin to worry about our physical condition until we notice what we are doing and direct our minds elsewhere.

Some students find themselves fixating on erotic images during meditation. We advise them to treat these images like any others: Notice them without judgment, then return to the meditation.

Obsession during meditation is very common. A painful relationship or an upsetting situation fills our minds and won't go away. Or we spiral downwards in obsessive self-criticism. Or we obsessively plan our day's activities. All of these obsessions temporarily get in the way of meditation. But this is just part of the process: Over time we become better acquainted with how our minds work, and we learn to deal with this meditative malaise by acknowledging our thoughts and returning again and again to the meditation.

Occasionally, people will experience deep feelings about events in their lives during meditation and begin to weep. This is entirely acceptable. As we get in touch with the pain we carry, we can't disregard it as easily as we ordinarily do. But the wave of despair or grief or sadness does not last. If you accept and appreciate its existence instead of fighting against it, it will dissipate on its own accord.

In the end, most people don't have extreme highs or extreme lows during meditation. The nature of the practice is less dramatic than that. As one student says, "When I meditate, it seems that nothing much is happening. But I feel so much calmer. I feel peaceful. And afterwards, my life seems more centered and on the right track." This feeling of calmness, then, is probably the most common mind-state that comes from meditation.

We cannot conclude our discussion about meditative experience without mentioning resistance. All meditators go through periods when they find themselves resisting meditation. Even though they sincerely want to do it, they "forget" about it, or they put it off until later, or they suddenly decide they can't meditate. The challenge of resistance is great, but it can teach us a great deal. We will discuss this phenomenon in greater detail later in the book.

How Does the Mind Work?

The nature of the mind is to think. During our waking hours our minds are constantly going, even though we usually don't pay attention to the content.

Our waking minds are like music that never stops. Sometimes the beat is fast and jagged, and other times it is slow and rhythmic. The pace and content change. The sound can even subside for the shortest moment, like the pause at the end of a musical phrase. But then it begins again.

The mind thinks only one thought at a time. Just as music unfolds by producing sound after sound, so too the mind's thoughts take place in sequence. All within a few seconds I might consider: I need to water my ficus plant; my chest cold seems to be getting better; I love that blue print on the wall; I hope my daughter can drop by tonight. All these thoughts tumble into my consciousness one after another.

Sometimes I have "something on my mind." That is, many of my thoughts are organized around and related to a particular subject. Still, each thought is a discrete entity that exists alone and is followed immediately by another.

Our feelings are very much affected by our thoughts. If a lot of negative thoughts are going through my mind, I probably feel depressed, anxious, or angry. Likewise, on days when my mind chatters away happily, I feel loving or contented.

It is important to note that the reverse is also true: When I feel unhappy, my thoughts are more negative. And when I am in a good mood, my thoughts tend to be positive.

Another characteristic of the mind is that it can observe its own workings. Most of us have not developed this skill.

Instead, our minds ramble from subject to subject, and we don't even notice. But we have the capacity to become aware of our thoughts and reflect on them.

Beginning meditators often feel that they are at the mercy of their minds. They've never considered the idea that they can help to shape or direct the content of their thoughts. We can learn to be aware of its workings and to become proficient in directing it. This is one of the tasks of meditation.

Is Jewish Meditation Dangerous?

Most of us want to expand the spiritual boundaries of our lives, but we are wary of doing anything that might threaten our well-being. Thus we approach Jewish meditation with care.

Jewish meditation, as I teach it, is safe, as long as it is practiced in a responsible way. Most people can do it without concern. However, it shouldn't be attempted by anyone in the midst of a mental health crisis. People who are psychotic, suicidal, or severely depressed are best off trying to stabilize themselves in more carefully supervised settings. Likewise, those who have difficulty staying oriented, or who have a tenuous hold on their lives, should not try to meditate right now.

As a teacher, I am careful to lead students into meditations that are within their psychic capacities. All of the meditations in this book, for example, have been done by large numbers of beginners with no known negative results.

The point of meditation is to develop spiritual consciousness over time, not to become flooded with too much, too soon. If you feel uneasy about a meditation that is being taught in a class or a workshop, don't do it. You can always sit quietly, focusing on your breath while others in the room try it. Likewise, skip any meditation in this book that doesn't seem appropriate for you.

Certain signs warn us that we should stop a meditation. One of them is pushing too hard. Another is generalized emotionality. If you find yourself overcome with extreme emotion that seems to have no base, the meditation might not be right for you. This state is different from the waves of sadness, grief, and despair that I mentioned earlier. Here you are caught up in an intense emotional whirlwind, and you feel lost in it. At such times it is useful to put aside the meditation and sit quietly, or simply watch your breath. Feel the ground beneath you. Physical contact with others can be helpful. Afterwards, you might want to talk with someone about your experience.

On days when you feel especially vulnerable or fragile, go easy. You might not want to try out new meditations unless they seem right for you. If you are meditating alone, choose a meditation that you've experienced in the past as calming and restorative. You will discover several meditations in this book that are good for these times.

As a beginning meditator, you have control over your practice. You can pick and chose those meditations that suit you. Any that feel scary or threatening should not be included on your list, even if other people like them. By fine-tuning your practice in this way, you will be on firm ground.

Most people never have any difficulties. In fact, I've been pleased to discover how safe the practice is. In my years as a teacher, I've been impressed by the large numbers of meditators who thrive on the practice, becoming emotionally more stable.

We return once again to the breath.
Begin by breathing deeply.

Let your breath out with a sound, as
you've done before.

Experience your body releasing the
tension you are holding.
Let the sound carry it away.

Do this several times.
Now, breathe in your usual way.

Watch your breath as it fills your
lungs.
Watch as your body expands to
receive it.
Then notice your chest contract as
your breath begins to depart.
Notice your body release it.
Keep your mind on your breath.
If your mind begins to wander, bring
it back.
Pay attention.
The breath flows in. The breath flows
out.

Continue this way for two or three minutes. You will become more settled and your mind will begin to quiet. Let yourself sink into this state. Become nourished by it.

Afterwards, take a few deep breaths, stretch, and return to the book.

4
Forms of Jewish Meditation

Through the centuries a great variety of Jewish meditations have been created. Beginning students often become confused by all the possibilities. They wonder how these meditations are similar and how are they different, and if some are better than others. Which should they use to start their practice?

I've found it helpful to divide Jewish meditations into three categories: focused meditations, awareness meditations, and emptiness meditations. These groups are determined by what the meditation does and how it does it. Within each category we find simple meditations and advanced meditations. There is no hierarchy, as meditations in all the groups can lead to a state of greater spiritual awareness and connection with the Divine.

What Are Focused Meditations?

In focused meditations the meditator concentrates on a single point. This point can be the breath, a word or phrase, a Jewish symbol, an image, or a sound.

Hundreds of focused meditations exist, each with a different focal point, and more are being created today. All have one thing in common: Their content is connected to the Jewish tradition.

We begin a focused meditation by bringing our attention to a single point. If the meditation specifies a Hebrew word, for example, we might repeat it silently, or visualize the letters, or experience the meaning of the word.

After settling into the meditation, our minds inevitably begin to wander. One thought leads to another until we notice what we are doing. Then we gently bring our attention back to the focus, and the process begins all over again.

Focused meditations sound simple, but they require great effort. Most people are surprised by the difficulty of keeping their minds focused even for a minute. When they discover that their thoughts have wandered yet again despite their best intentions, they realize anew that they have little control over their mental processes.

We encourage students simply to notice without judgment what they have been thinking, when their minds wander. In the Hasidic tradition every thought that comes into consciousness during meditation is considered to contain a spark of Divinity, even if it is negative or perverse.

The aim of focused meditation is to focus the mind on a single point. Over time, people build up the ability to do this for longer periods, although even seasoned meditators sometimes have "off" days when their thoughts wander ceaselessly.

Focused meditations benefit us in several ways. We cannot help but be affected by the experience of concentrating on something that is spiritually connected. Thirty minutes of meditation in the morning on *chesed,* or Divine lovingkindness, will radiate through the rest of the day, even if our minds refuse to stay fixed on *chesed* most of the time while we meditate.

Another benefit of focused meditations is that we develop the ability to notice where our minds go when they wander. We learn more about what is "on our minds." And we discover how to put aside these preoccupations, at least for a while, and direct our attention back to the task at hand.

These are the most obvious outcomes of focused meditation. But a more subtle one exists. Sometimes meditators experience an "open space" around the single point on which they are focusing. Here they become deeply connected with God in a state of *devekut.* Or they become one with the Holy, so that the separate self dissolves into a state of nonduality. This spiritual experience, like any other, is transitory, but it can be profound.

Focused meditations are the backbone of Jewish meditation. If we consider the meditations that were developed in previous centuries, we find that most fall into this category. Whether they involve visualizing Hebrew words or rearranging the letters of the Divine Name, they follow the same pattern. The *yod-hay-vav-hay* meditation taught later in this book, for instance, is a Kabbalistic focused meditation.

Many contemporary Jewish meditations also belong within this group. They have been created by meditation teachers, and they are based on meaningful Jewish symbols, images, or words. The first meditation you will learn, the *hineini* meditation, is an example of this.

What Are Awareness Meditations?

During awareness meditation the mind is allowed to wander freely without a focus. Thoughts emerge one after another, and their flow is uninterrupted. The meditator simply observes them, names them, and notices their contents.

The aim of awareness meditation is to become more

aware of our mental processes. We develop this ability over time by observing our thoughts. Once we have the skill, we can extend our awareness beyond the mind to the world around us and the spiritual realm.

At first glance this kind of meditation seems much easier than focused meditation since the mind is not required to stay on one subject. But don't be fooled by this apparent ease: Many people find it harder to track their thoughts if there is no focus. They say it's like trying to grab hold of sand slipping through their fingers.

Within our minds we have an "observer self." The observer self notices what is going on and names thoughts and feelings. This is the internal voice that says, "Oh, I am worrying about my father," or "Oh, I am obsessing about the pain in my belly," or "Oh, I feel joyous at this moment." The observer self does not analyze these observations. It only identifies them.

In our everyday lives the observer self is usually "asleep," and our thoughts jump from subject to subject without awareness. This is what happens during most of our waking hours. But in awareness meditation the observer self is called into action. At first it can hardly keep up with the powerful stream of thought. But like a body that is exercised over time, it becomes more adept, and we learn to notice the barely visible shifts of thought and mood without analyzing them.

One of the great benefits of awareness meditation is that the observer self becomes strengthened. As we become increasingly aware of our thoughts, we know ourselves better, and our mental processes become more familiar to us. We have more information about our positive and negative qualities so that we can do the self-refinement described earlier in the book.

Awareness meditation also teaches us that our thoughts are not permanent. They are like waves rising and falling on the shore of our consciousness, then receding back into the vast ocean. This impermanence startles many of us, because we assume that thought is more concrete than it really is. We usually identify with what goes through our minds. If we have angry thoughts, we consider ourselves to be angry people; if we have positive thoughts, we think of ourselves as optimistic.

We soon observe in awareness meditation, however, that our thoughts come and go, and that we are separate from them. We realize that we are fluid beings. As part of the great cosmos of creation, we are changing constantly. This understanding can lead to a feeling of spiritual unity with all life, and a deeper connection with the Holy.

Many people wonder why awareness meditation is considered to be Jewish since it appears to resemble Buddhist mindfulness practice. But Buddhism does not have a copyright on awareness. The Jewish meditative tradition also embraces the understanding that awareness begins within the mind and leads to greater spiritual consciousness and a connection with God.

In Jewish awareness practice, meditators often are instructed to silently repeat a Hebrew word or phrase when they notice where their minds have gone. This addition strengthens the practice and connects it even more to Judaism. The *gam zeh kadosh* awareness meditation, included in this book, is an example of this practice.

Awareness meditation is far less common than focused meditation in Judaism. Still, many people find it useful, and interest in it is growing. More than any other, it gives us a skill that transfers over into our everyday lives: the ability to pay attention to our experience and to the world around us.

What Are Emptiness Meditations?

Emptiness meditation seeks to empty the mind of all thought. It does this by quieting the mental processes so that we enter into a deep silence, a state of "not-thinking."

Nobody can stay in this meditative state for long, because the nature of the mind is to think. But we can begin to find the spaciousness between our thoughts, and experience moments when our minds are still. Over time we can learn to prolong these moments so that we become familiar with the state of nothingness, or *ayin,* as it is called in Judaism.

Emptiness meditations usually start with the meditator stilling the mind through focusing on the breath. Then the movement into emptiness begins, guided by a meditation designed for this purpose. As all thought drops away, the meditator simply exists in a state of nothingness. The familiar mental activities no longer take place. The observer self—which we work so hard to develop in awareness meditations—is put to rest.

However, the mind begins its chatter sooner or later, and the meditator immediately is propelled back into the world of thought. The task then is to notice where the mind has gone, as with the other kinds of meditation, and return once again to the state of emptiness.

The experience of *ayin* cannot be described. By its very definition it is beyond language. However, many people report that they feel enormously renewed after this form of meditation. The hardships of their daily lives no longer seem so overwhelming, and all life is experienced as interconnected. They say they have lost the feeling of being a separate being, and this gives them equanimity.

This shift in internal reality stays with them and is one of the great benefits of emptiness meditation. We come to understand that *ayin* is not dead nothingness, but cosmic possibility. Although nothing is formed in this state, and nothing is there, it is charged with creative potential.

Emptiness meditation has been practiced through the centuries, although it is far less common than focused meditation. In the past only very experienced meditators were taught to do it. Because it is difficult, we encourage students first to establish a strong practice in focused and awareness meditation.

Which Meditations Are Best for You?

Each group of meditations offers something special, and the techniques, although related, differ in significant ways.

Meditators report that they have powerful experiences of the silence within by using meditations from each of these groups. One group is not "better" or "higher" than another: They all are pathways to spiritual consciousness, and they can help you transcend the duality of everyday life.

I strongly advise beginning meditators to start with focused meditations. They are a good way to become familiar with the workings of the mind, which most people know little about. They also help to develop the ability to concentrate, an important aspect in being able to have deeper spiritual experiences.

Many beginning meditators find that focused meditations ground them in the Jewish context of meditation. As they learn to focus on Hebrew words, or the names of the Divine, or images from the tradition, they begin to feel more comfortable with the roots of the practice. This is especially important for people who have had little Jewish education, or who feel conflicted about their involvement with Judaism.

Once you become experienced in focused meditation, you can begin to explore awareness meditation. But you should not jump into it too quickly, as it can create confusion. It is too easy to move back and forth between the old practice and the new, and end up doing neither very well. Take your time. Then, after you become firmly established in both kinds of meditation, you can move on to emptiness meditation.

With experience, people usually become adept in doing meditations from all three groups. They draw from the store-house of possibilities, tailor their practices to suit their temperaments and spiritual needs.

But most meditators eventually discover that one meditation, or one group of meditations, works best for them. I know people who prefer emptiness meditation above the others because it helps them quiet their minds. Others reach a state of spiritual openness by focusing on a single image. Still others find that they grow spiritually and feel most connected to all creation by having a daily practice of awareness meditation.

What about Chanting and Singing?

I've described Jewish meditation as a contemplative practice where you sit, alone or with other people, and silently go inward. But within the Jewish tradition other possibilities exist, such as chanting sacred words or phrases and singing *niggunim* (wordless melodies).

Historically, these practices have been used to increase spiritual connection. Teachers today disagree about whether they are part of Jewish meditation. I discuss them here, however, because many people find that they add an important dimension to their meditative practices.

Chanting and singing follow the same form as focused meditation. When you chant a line from liturgy, the sounds and the words are the focal point. Or when you sing a *niggun* over and over again, your attention is placed on the reverberating sound. Thus, you focus on a single point outside the self.

In Jewish meditation we chant sacred words or sing *nig-*

gunim in a meditative way. The idea is to let the sound fill your entire consciousness. As you merge with the sound, all extraneous thought disappears. However, your mind will begin to wander, even with this strong a focus. So you bring it back again to the chant or *niggun,* just as you do with other focused meditations.

I've just described how chants and *niggunim* can be used as meditation. In reality, people in Jewish settings sometimes sing *niggunim* in a more casual way, as though they are sitting around a campfire. They enjoy the beautiful melodies and the group camaraderie—but this is not meditation.

At the center where I teach we often begin our meditation groups with a *niggun* or a chant. Many people find this to be the easiest way to enter meditation because it "jump starts" them into a more contemplative state. After chanting or singing together for several minutes, we then move into a long silent meditation. The silence, we've found, is even more potent after singing together.

Teachers of meditation introduce chants and *niggunim* in different ways: Some never use them, others occasionally alternate them with silent meditation, and still others teach them to the exclusion of more contemplative meditations.

In recent years the practice of chants and *niggunim* has been growing. New chants are being written, with words drawn from Jewish liturgy and the Bible. Many *niggunim* from past centuries—especially those found in Hasidism—are being reclaimed. More meditators are becoming familiar with this meditative practice.

In this book I've concentrated on contemplative meditation because it is difficult to teach chants and *niggunim* on the written page. But I also believe that contemplative meditation is the core of Jewish meditation. Nothing takes the place of sitting silently and learning to guide your mind to the vast territory within. Other, more expressive meditative practices can supplement this and at times take precedence over it, but we always come back to this primary practice.

What about Walking and Movement Meditations?

Some current teachers have brought walking meditation into Jewish practice. They usually intersperse it with sitting meditation so that students sit, then walk, then sit, then walk. They add it to Jewish meditation because it helps raise consciousness about our physical experience and the world in which we live.

In this kind of meditation people move very, very slowly in a prescribed area. It might take ten minutes to cover ten feet. The aim of walking meditation is to become more aware; in this regard it is like other awareness meditations. However, the field of observation extends beyond the workings of the mind to the body or to those things within our view.

If we are concentrating on our bodies, we pay attention to the soles of our feet as they touch the ground, the lift in our chest as we inhale, the swing of our arms. Each of us is a part of the natural world, and our tiniest movements are like water slipping over stones. As we move in this slow rhythm, we experience ourselves as infused with Divine energy.

Or if we are using this meditation to become more aware of the world around us, we pay special attention to everything we see. Walking in the same slow way, we take the time to look—*really* look—at the objects around us. As we observe their lines, shapes, and colors, we are filled with the beauty and richness of the universe in which we live.

We don't find specific references to walking meditation in Jewish texts. But we take the liberty of borrowing it from other meditative traditions because it fits within a Jewish framework and increases our effectiveness as meditators. I don't teach walking meditation often, but I find it useful, especially when people are sitting for many long hours during retreats. It provides a break in pace and helps energize weary meditators.

We've all heard that Jews are most comfortable in their heads. Judaism is not known for its wisdom about the body or for its interest in movement. But some teachers have combined yoga with Jewish meditation to develop new forms. Others have created the practice of *otiot chayyot* (slow meditative movements in which the meditator physically takes on the shape of Hebrew letters). This practice did not exist in past centuries, as far as we know, but it draws upon the Kabbalah's mystical understanding of Hebrew letters. Clearly it falls within the boundaries of Jewish meditative practice as it is done today. Like the Eastern practice of tai chi, this intricate set of body motions is an art. Steady concentration is demanded and the mind is instructed to focus entirely upon the movement.

What about Guided Visualization?

Many people think that guided visualization is part of Jewish meditation. Before we go any further, I want to clear up this misconception.

In guided visualization the leader or teacher usually begins by asking the participants to imagine they are having a certain experience, or they are in a certain place. Once they are "there," the teacher leads them through an unfolding of the imagination. Each step of the way is accompanied by a few minutes of silence, so that the participants have time to fully imagine what the teacher has suggested. The structured visualization reaches a climax—and hopefully, a moment of revelation—before it is concluded.

The task of the leader is to skillfully bring the participants along on the journey of the guided visualization. The task of the participants is to follow the instructions and open their imaginations to what is suggested.

This experience can be extremely powerful. But it is not meditation. Even if the story line of the guided visualization is built around Jewish symbols or images ("Imagine that you are lighting the Shabbat candles, and suddenly you see a blue light around them. Now imagine that you sit by these candles in a darkened room. . . ."), it is still not Jewish meditation. Why? Because the process is different. Guided visualizations are designed to lead participants to a specific experience, not to the silence within.

Where Does Prayer Fit In?

Beginning meditators often are confused by the similarities between prayer and Jewish meditation. The two spiritual practices look alike because both of them are reflective. We go "within" during both of them. Even though many Jewish prayers are said in the plural—"We beseech you" instead of "I beseech you"—they are meant to express the feelings within each of us. And meditation, as we have said, is directed to the silence within.

Prayer and meditation also are similar in that they can be done alone or with others. Even though Jewish prayer traditionally takes place in a gathering of ten or more people, it is considered legitimate to pray by yourself. Meditation too can be a solo practice.

Both prayer and meditation appear to be directed toward a connection with God. But a closer look reveals a major difference between them. In prayer the intention is to communicate directly with the Divine. We approach God thoughtfully and with respect, but we are actively reaching out. Whether it be through words of praise, or blessing, or thankfulness, or speaking directly, we voice what is in our hearts, and God is said to receive our prayers.

In Jewish prayer we use a *siddur,* a prayer book. The prayers include selected psalms and writings compiled through the centuries. They follow a prescribed order, and only a small amount of time is set aside for personal prayer. Our task is to align ourselves with the words of the service and infuse them with meaning so that we are not mechanically repeating them but praying from our most vulnerable and revealed selves.

In Jewish meditation we do not attempt to communicate directly with God. We follow certain techniques to move into a spiritually open state, and then we experience whatever is there. This may include directly sensing God's presence. Or it may not. Years can go by without having this experience, even a lifetime, yet meditation will still be valuable and life altering.

In the end we say that these two practices differ because prayer and meditation are distinctly different activities. Each has its own techniques and its own content. Yet they can be combined in many ways, as you will see in chapter 9. People find that this makes both practices even more powerful.

What about the Breath?

The breath is used as a focusing device in most meditative traditions. To the surprise of many Jews, it also is central in Jewish meditation.

Meditation teachers introduce the breath in a variety of ways. Although a few like to focus on it for the entire meditation period, most teachers prefer to use it for a few minutes at the beginning of a longer meditation. This is done because it helps meditators settle into a quiet state.

All of the core meditations in this book start by first taking several deep breaths and making a sound with each exhalation, just as you have done in the previous chapters. You will feel yourself begin to let go of your everyday concerns as you do this. Then you will resume your ordinary breathing. As you watch its rise and fall, paying attention only to the breath, you will feel a quietness begin to descend over you. Within a minute or two you will be ready to move into the longer core meditation.

The breath, then, acts as a bridge between everyday life and the longer meditation. It functions like a chant or a *niggun* in that it helps to "jump start" the meditative process.

I like to teach my students about the special mystical qualities of the breath. In Genesis we are told that God breathed into *ha-adam,* the first human on earth, and made *ha-adam* a living being. This most intimate of acts, the transfer of Divine breath to the human, is interpreted to mean that all life is dependent on the breath of the Divine.

Also, the word for "breath" in Hebrew, *neshimah,* is almost the same as one of the words for "soul," *neshamah.* Thus the breath and the soul are seen in Judaism as closely related, both gifts coming from God. The breath contains soul-energy, and the soul is like a breath, filling us and then returning to the Source.

In the morning prayer service, one of the prayers says: *Nishmat kol chai, y'varech et-shimha, Adonai Eloheinu*, "Let the breath of all life bless God." This prayer expresses the holiness of our breath. Not only do we receive the gift of breath from the Divine, but we contribute to the blessing of God through our breath/soul.

Can Meditation from Other Traditions Be Integrated into Jewish Meditation?

Jewish meditation, as we have seen, is porous. Throughout the centuries it has absorbed certain ideas and techniques from other traditions, and it continues to do so.

We have a lot to learn about the meditative process. Buddhism and Hinduism, for example, are more sophisticated and knowledgeable about the different stages of meditation than Judaism. They have identified the obstacles more clearly and devised ways to approach them. If we ignore their wisdom, we miss an important opportunity to deepen Jewish meditation.

Boundaries exist, however. To keep the integrity of Jewish meditation, we integrate only those practices that build on what we already have. They must fit within our philosophy and theology. A simple walking awareness meditation is fine because we can teach it in a Jewish context. But a Christian meditation on the Holy Trinity is not transferable. We exclude anything from another tradition that is not consistent with the Jewish understanding of God. The biblical injunction "You shall pray to no other gods" is extended here to "You shall not meditate on other gods."

Many Jewish meditators have experienced non-Jewish meditation. Whether it be chanting for five years with a Sufi group, or practicing Vipassana meditation for twenty-five years, they begin Jewish meditation as seasoned meditators. We encourage them to build on their past meditative experience rather than disavow it, because they've already acquired skills that will help them learn Jewish meditation.

But some students are not interested, at least at first, in taking on Jewish meditation. They're satisfied with their well-established Buddhist or Hindu practices. They come to the center where I teach because they want to meditate in a Jewish context or learn more about Jewish mysticism and Judaism.

We welcome them to practice with us, even if their meditation differs from ours. We respect their desire for a connection to Judaism, and we appreciate the wisdom they often bring to our discussions about the process of meditation.

5
Getting Started

I've occasionally been at meetings or services where the leader says, "Let's take a few minutes to meditate together." The people around me close their eyes and I always wonder what is going through their minds. Some, I assume, draw on their already established meditation practices, but others must feel bewildered. I know I did before I began to meditate.

If we are told to meditate without being taught what to do, our minds continue with their ordinary thoughts. We might appreciate the few minutes of silence, but we wonder why this is considered to be a worthwhile activity. Isn't it just the same old mental whirl?

Meditation is a skill: We have to learn how to do it.

Students always ask a lot of questions about the mechanics of meditation. Sometimes they voice them hesitantly because they fear sounding silly or stupid. But most meditation teachers are pleased to answer them. Everyone needs help in grasping the complexities. People can be misinformed about the smallest detail, and this will affect their experiences as meditators in surprisingly significant ways.

Until now, we have approached Jewish meditation in a theoretical way. This has been crucial beginning information.

But now we are ready to move on to the rudiments of the practice. Some of you might be tempted to jump over the practical details in this chapter. Or you might assume that they are less important than the material discussed earlier. Or you may be impatient to start meditating.

Please take the time to read this material carefully so that you are grounded in the practicalities of Jewish meditation. If you absorb these details before you actually begin to meditate, your practice will go more smoothly. At the very least, you won't have to rush back to this chapter, wondering what went wrong and how you can fix it.

Should You Meditate Alone or with Others?

Most of us think of Judaism as a community-based religion. Certain parts of synagogue prayer cannot even begin before a *minyan* of ten people has gathered. As a result, we might think that meditating alone is wrong, or even forbidden.

This impression is mistaken. Solitary practice is central to Jewish meditation. Pragmatically, most of us cannot find people to meditate with on a regular basis, so we have to do it alone, at least part of the time. But also, the practice thrives in this setting. We can pace it according to our own rhythms, and it becomes an integral part of our days. We're more likely to take responsibility for it if it is up to us to make sure it continues.

Group meditation can be useful, however. When twenty meditators sit quietly together, a potent atmosphere fills the room. People often find that their meditative experience is heightened in this setting. Meditating with others also reinforces discipline. If I regularly attend a Wednesday morning meditation group, I can count on meditating at least once a week. Getting myself to do it on other days, then, may not be so daunting.

Meditation can be a lonely practice, especially if you don't have anyone to talk with about it. Meditation groups provide you with the opportunity to get to know people who understand and appreciate your experience.

We learn from each other. I've always found it useful to hear from group members about the self-refinement they are doing through meditation, and the highs and lows of their practices. If I am isolated, I too easily slip into grandiosity, considering myself to be more enlightened than I actually am. Or I think I am the only one struggling with restlessness, or inattention, or sleepiness, or physical pain.

Talking with others provides us with a good reality check. I suggest you join an already established group, or start one yourself if you can. Or at least look for another person with whom you can share your experience.

In the end, however, groups are limited in what they can do. Meditation is an individual practice. Even if you do it with others, you are moving into the silence within yourself. A group can support you and give you courage in this effort, but only you can accomplish it. Ultimately, you are on your own.

The rest of this chapter is about individual meditative practice. You will learn what you need to meditate alone. When you arrange to meditate with a group, then, you can draw from this material and adapt it for your own use.

Where Should You Meditate?

I once knew a student who had a great desire to meditate. But every time he tried it, he began to itch all over and couldn't sit still. In session after session, he became discouraged and self-critical.

One weekend he drove by himself to the most beautiful mountain he knew, three hundred miles from home. He hiked into the wilderness to a huge white rock. The day was sunny and warm, and he was surrounded by scrub brush and alpine wildflowers. Surely this was the perfect setting for him to overcome his meditation difficulties.

After a quick lunch he sat on the rock and began to meditate. It seemed to work—at first. Amazingly, his body did not itch. But something else caught his attention: a buzzing sound. He tried to ignore it, but he couldn't. Opening one eye, he saw a big fly circling around his head. He swatted at it, but the buzzing sound continued. And continued. And continued. Until he finally got up and left.

This story points out that there are always distractions in meditation. They can be internal, like itches or cramps; or they can be external, like buzzing noises. Meditators discover ways to work with internal distractions. They also need to consider how to deal with those that are external.

Some people think they have to find a place without noise in order to meditate. But such places do not exist. Have you ever gone outside on a summer's night, or sat in the quietest room in your house, only to discover how much noise there actually is in that place?

It's clear that you will have to deal with extraneous sound wherever you meditate. Over time, you will learn to direct your attention away from it so that you don't become distracted.

Still, some noises are worse than others. There used to be an especially loud clock in my living room near my meditation chair. I liked the way it looked on the mantle, with its green face and black hands, but its tick-tock, tick-tock often distracted me when I was meditating. One day, my meditation partner asked if we could put the clock away before we began. I somehow hadn't thought of that before. The house was now so much more peaceful. I still heard the sound of the birds outside, the hum of the refrigerator, and the squeal of brakes, but I no longer had to struggle with that infuriating clock.

When choosing a place to meditate, pick your sounds with care. Don't sit near something that you know will irritate you. You can make your environment more conducive by turning off the phone so its ringing won't disrupt you. And turn off your computer too, if its hum is going to remind you of all the work left to do.

Many of us live in households with partners, kids, or friends. I meditate now in my living room—my husband meditates with me—but when I lived with nonmeditators, I practiced on a cushion in the far corner of the bedroom, which was the quietest place in the house.

Your housemates will not necessarily understand or respect your need for quiet when you meditate. A closed door can seem like a rejection, and a request for silence can seem like rigidity. You have the difficult task of finding an adequate space for yourself without upsetting others over your new practice.

This can be a challenge. I've found that it's best to explain what you are doing when you meditate, and why you've taken it up. Your practice will be less threatening to your housemates. Perhaps you can arrange a tradeoff with one of them: If you are assured quiet time to meditate, you will return the favor by taking over a household job or doing something special for that person.

Hopefully, you can meditate at home. But if there are too many distractions to allow that, consider taking the time to meditate at your workplace or in your parked car. Parents with small children especially should try this. I know many people who go to work twenty or thirty minutes early, while it's still quiet. Or they manage to meditate in between clients or tasks during the day.

Wherever you meditate, it is important to sit in the same place each time. This helps settle you into your practice. The big white chair in my living room is my spot. I've meditated there for many years, so that when I pass by it, I am reminded of my practice. And when I sit there to meditate, I feel ready to begin.

People often ask if they should reserve a special room or a special corner for meditation. This is useful but not necessary. Most of us have space limitations. My chair doubles as a seat for friends and a spot for me to read in the evenings. Even so, it is indisputably my place of meditation.

When you chose where to meditate, pay attention to aesthetics. Is the room beautiful, or at least pleasing to you? If something in the environment is offensive, cover it up, or move it, or find another place to meditate. Even though your eyes are closed during meditation, you will feel more comfortable in surroundings that don't jar your sensibilities.

Consider the light where you meditate. Is it soothing? When I first moved into my house, I put my white chair directly in front of a huge window. But the light was too strong there and I had to pull it back, away from the sunlight.

Make sure that your meditation spot feels right for you. Each location has its own subtle energy, and it affects you more than you usually realize. Try sitting in several different places—and even moving the furniture around, if necessary—until you find the spot that makes you sigh, "Yes, this is it."

What Should the Physical Arrangement Be for Meditation?

Once you've chosen a place to meditate, you need to decide how to set it up.

The intrepid among you might want to sit directly on the floor in what is known as the lotus position, with one leg crossed over the other. But everyone else will need a meditation cushion or a chair.

You should find someplace to sit that is relatively

comfortable. In Jewish meditation, nobody gets points for physical hardship. A low stack of cushions on the floor can be easier on your body than just one, or a floor seat with a backrest may work better than cushions. Some people prefer to use meditation "benches." When I teach I like to settle on top of three cushions because it causes the least amount of strain on my troublesome knee. If you sit on a hard floor, you probably need something under your ankle bones as they can press into the surface when your legs are crossed. A rug or a soft cloth under your feet can help with this.

For those of you who meditate in chairs, look for one that supports you without causing you to slouch. In my white chair I sit up straight. The chair is deep enough so that I'm not even tempted to lean against the back. Otherwise, it probably wouldn't work because I'd sink into the soft cushions. In the past I meditated on a hard wooden chair. I liked it because it supported my back, and it was short enough so that my feet rested flat on the floor.

You'll find that the dimensions of the chair are important in giving you comfort. It shouldn't be too tall or too deep. Some people like the seat to be padded.

As you can see, many possibilities exist. Do your best to find a place to sit that works for you. If you have physical problems that preclude using a meditation cushion on the floor, don't be concerned. Meditators are not rated according to where or how they sit. If they were, some of our finest teachers would be considered failures.

Sometimes I am asked if it is okay to set up a meditation altar as part of the physical arrangement. You might know someone who has done this. One of my Buddhist friends has an altar that she changes from month to month. She covers it with a colorful cloth on which she arranges pictures of her teachers or other significant people, flowers, stones, a statue of Buddha, and a figurine of Kwan Yin, the Buddhist goddess of compassion. Before meditating, she sometimes prays to Kwan Yin and draws strength from the other objects.

Jews traditionally don't have altars, but if you wish, you can bring objects that have special meaning to you to your meditation space. For example, many people like keeping a shofar (a ram's horn, traditionally blown during the High Holy Days) close by. Or you can surround yourself with natural objects, such as flowers or rocks. The point is not to worship these items or to pray to them—in Judaism that's considered idolatry—but to experience their presence as a gift of the Divine.

How Should You Sit During Meditation?

The Jewish tradition says little about posture during meditation. Many teachers—especially those with Buddhist backgrounds—encourage people to sit with their spines straight. In this position it is easier to stay alert to the task of meditation. The breath enters with fewer obstacles, and the body is under less strain than if it is allowed to slump.

People often begin meditating in a straight position, but as the minutes go by, their backs slowly curve and their chests collapse. Soon they look like they're about ready to fall over. Teachers usually instruct them to notice what is happening with their bodies while meditating so that they can correct this tendency.

Beginning meditators sometimes sit with their arms crossed, or they sling one leg over the other, or they cross their hands. This posture is not conducive to meditation. We encourage people to separate their arms, unclasp their hands, and put both feet on the floor. That way, they are in a more open position. The only exception is for those sitting in a lotus or half-lotus position on a pillow or the floor.

People often ask us what to do with their hands during meditation. Those who have had experience in other meditative traditions often prefer to place their palms upwards. This is acceptable, but no better than keeping the palms facedown. Some meditators like to rest their hands close to their lower belly. Others keep them on their thighs. Whatever you do, make sure that the position feels easy to you and doesn't strain your body.

The rule of thumb about posture is that there should be no extra holding or tension in the body while you sit. If there is, relax or change positions. You are perfectly free to move during meditation. A leg that is falling asleep should be shifted rather than kept in a painful position. The only requirement is to move quietly when you are sitting with others.

If you've had experience with Zen Buddhism, the Jewish approach to posture might seem undisciplined to you. But we've found that it works well for what we are trying to accomplish. As long as the body is comfortable but alert, you can focus on the work of meditation.

Despite this more lenient approach, however, many people experience physical aches and pains during Jewish meditation. They find that sitting in chairs or on the floor for a long time isn't easy. The headache or aching back that they've tried all day to ignore suddenly looms in their consciousness. Body pain can be a big distraction during meditation. It should be handled in the same way that we handle other distractions: Become aware of it, name it without judgment, and then return to the meditation.

Other body sensations, such as twitching, cramping, or itching, also distract meditators. If you find yourself shifting restlessly or scratching your body often during a session, try to settle back into the meditation. Some teachers encourage students to remain still at these times rather than giving in to the impulse to move. If you do this, you will learn that these annoying body sensations come and go. Like thoughts, they are impermanent.

Every so often people ask if they can meditate lying down. This is permissible. But since it is easy to fall asleep in this position, we don't encourage it. In a meditation group I once taught, a man regularly stretched out on a cushion and began to snore. It was hard to see what he was getting out of the experience, but he kept returning. Finally, he surprised us by sitting up with everyone else. When asked why he had changed his routine, he said that he guessed he was ready to meditate.

In the last two decades we've learned a lot about the connection between body and spirit. A tense body does not welcome spiritual experience. But neither does a sprawled, sleeping body.

Should You Meditate If You Are in a Bad Mood or Having a Crisis?

The answer to this question is yes—with some exceptions. Once you begin a meditation practice, it is best to continue it on a regular basis. Certainly a bad mood shouldn't stop you. If you are irritable or depressed, go ahead and meditate.

Many people find that meditation helps them with their everyday mood swings. I've frequently had the experience of feeling grouchy when I start a session, but becoming much calmer as I meditate. Meditation gives us emotional distance from the irritations that grind us down. I feel less upset about a problem at work or a difficult relationship after I've spent thirty minutes focusing on the healing light of the Divine Presence.

I'm not saying that meditation is easy when I am in a bad mood. I find myself obsessing about those things that bother me, and I have to remember to return to the meditation again and again. My wandering mind frustrates me. Still, I find it worth the effort.

States of crisis are a more complicated matter. If you are faced with a relationship breakup or the death of someone close to you, you probably will not be able to meditate at first. You'll be too absorbed in your own emotional process. But when you resume your practice, meditation can help you acknowledge your grief and see your loss from a larger perspective.

If you are ill or faced with chronic illness, I encourage you to try to meditate. It can give you the strength to continue in your life. And if you are struggling with a problem such as unemployment, meditation can help ground you. We all go through times when our lives seem to be falling apart, and the discipline of a practice can give us stability.

But meditation is not appropriate for people who are in extreme mental health crises. Anyone who is contemplating suicide, or who is clinically depressed or psychotic, or who cannot function in daily life should stay away from the practice. If this is the state you are in, you need activities that connect you to the world around you and give you hope. Meditation is too solitary a path for you at this time. Once you are past your crisis, you can turn to it.

How Long Should You Meditate?

I recently told students in a beginning meditation class to set aside ten minutes each day for meditation. "Only ten minutes?" a woman said. "Surely that's not long enough!"

When people start meditating, ten minutes can seem endless. I'd prefer that they yearn for more meditation than be discouraged by too rigorous a sitting. A great deal can be accomplished in ten minutes. And if the sitting turns out to be too short, it can always be lengthened.

In meditation there is no "right" amount of time. Each meditator is different. I like to meditate for forty minutes, especially on Shabbat. This is my natural rhythm. On retreats, however, I can do it for hours if there are breaks for walking meditation or exercise. Sometimes in my busy life I have to settle for ten or fifteen minutes of meditation. Even though I prefer the longer sessions, I still appreciate these shorter sittings.

Most beginning meditators soon discover what's best for them. If you stop too soon, you don't get what you want from the practice; and if you sit too long, you reach the point of diminishing returns. Over the months ahead you will learn how much time you need.

For those of you who are starting a meditation practice, I suggest that you commit yourselves to ten minutes. If you wish, you can stretch it out longer. But do this carefully. Some beginners are so enthusiastic that they burn themselves out by taking on too strenuous a practice. Then they give up on the whole idea of meditation. Remember: You have the rest of your life in which to meditate. You don't have to cram it all in immediately.

How Often Should You Meditate?

I encourage beginning meditators to meditate every day. This will be easy for some of you, and you'll quickly develop the habit of slipping your practice into your daily routine.

But more likely, you will have difficulty. You'll find yourself chafing against the regularity of the practice. Meditation takes up precious time, and when it is added to the list of work responsibilities, exercise, child care, and relationship demands, it can seem like an impossibility. We already have too much to do and we don't welcome one more thing, even if it holds the promise of spiritual transformation.

Meditation takes time. There's no way around it. A commitment must be made to doing it, otherwise it won't happen.

Often people decide to begin meditating, but when the appointed hour arrives, they find reasons to avoid it. They're too tired. Or they're too involved in some other project. Or they're not in the mood. Or they decide they won't get anything out of it. Or they figure they can let it go until tomorrow or next week.

These are examples of resistance. Almost everybody experiences it in one form or another, especially in the beginning. Resistance is not bad. But it often confuses or upsets students. Why should they put off or avoid doing something they say they want to do? The only explanation they can find is that they are lazy, or uncommitted, or they've failed. This self-criticism makes them feel hopeless about the possibility of their success as meditators.

We tell our students to notice their resistance, but not to judge it. Self-criticism only makes them feel worse. If they have not been meditating regularly, they can begin again. And again.

At first, it takes a lot of determination to stick with a meditation practice. But as time goes by, it becomes easier. Meditators become accustomed to the results of meditation, and if they miss a day or two, they feel the lack of it. "I get tangled up when I don't meditate," one student said recently. "My life doesn't go as smoothly. Meditation is essential to my well-being, and it's no longer a choice."

The practice has its own momentum. If you can continue it long enough so that it becomes a part of your life, you eventually won't have to rely as much on your willpower.

What Time of Day Should You Meditate?

Many of us associate meditation with the morning. We picture early risers practicing diligently before everyone else gets up.

In Jewish meditation morning meditation is fine. But so is afternoon or evening meditation. There is no proper time to practice.

Some people prefer morning meditation because it's convenient. As one woman student says, "It's out of bed, onto the meditation bench, then into my day." She would have trouble fitting her practice into her schedule if she didn't do it first thing in the morning.

This student especially likes the feeling of morning meditation. For her it has some of the dreamy qualities of sleep. More than at any other time of day, she finds that she can meditate in a satisfying way. Her mind jumps around less, and she experiences an inner silence that dissipates once the day moves on.

But morning is difficult for many people. Another student has little children who demand a lot of attention when they wake up. She'd like to rise before they do and meditate, but she's usually too tired. Besides, she's most tense in the morning. The pressures of work flood her mind, and she's better off mobilizing herself to get out the front door than sitting quietly. From experience she knows that meditation works beautifully for her in the evening after the children are asleep. She loves the feeling of peace and stillness then, and she is in her most receptive state.

We're all different. Some people find it hard to sleep if they meditate just before bedtime; others don't. Depending on your schedule and your internal rhythms, you will need to select a time of day that suits you. You'll want to consider all the options. I used to think I was not a "morning person," but I've discovered that I like morning meditation. Still, the sweetest time for me is late afternoon, and that's when I practice these days.

Meditators do best if they make a commitment to meditate at a certain time every day. In the beginning, especially, this is crucial for stabilizing a practice. If left to your own devices, you too easily can skip over morning meditation, saying that you'll meditate later, and then skip over afternoon and evening meditation, saying that you'll meditate the next day. In the space of a week, you won't be meditating at all.

Making a decision about when to meditate helps build your practice. If you do it when you've said, you have the satisfaction of fulfilling your commitment. And if you've slipped, at least you know what time you'll be meditating tomorrow.

How Do You Track Time During Meditation?

Students often ask how to time their meditation sessions. When practicing with a group, this isn't a problem, because the leader watches the clock. But when people meditate alone, they have nobody to let them know when the time is up.

It's important to decide how you will track time before you begin a session. Some people set a timer, alarm clock, or clock radio. This lets them relax, knowing that when the buzzer rings or the music begins, the meditation time is over.

I prefer to put my watch in front of me because I like to end my meditation sessions in silence. After years of practice, my internal clock is highly calibrated and I don't have to check the time very often.

You can try glancing at your watch or clock every so often during a session. Even though this momentarily breaks the intensity of the meditation, you'll get used to it. This method is better than worrying the whole time that you'll be late to work.

If you are fortunate, a housemate can call you when your meditation time is over. But choose someone reliable; otherwise, you'll be wondering during the session if you will be forgotten.

What about the Breath During Meditation?

Jewish meditation does not tell us how we should breathe while we meditate. Over the years, however, I've found that most people prefer to inhale and exhale softly through their nostrils. Some, however, adopt the Hindu method of breathing in through the nose and breathing out through the mouth. A few breathe in and out through the mouth, the least effective method.

While meditating, it is best to breathe in your normal rhythm. You shouldn't take in more air than usual—except for a short time—because it might make you lightheaded. You can try experimenting with your breath. Take several deep breaths if you are sleepy or low in energy. This might help wake you up. Or exhale deeply a few times if your mind is agitated and you are having a hard time staying with the meditation.

Each core meditation in this book starts with a focus on the breath. You already have learned how to do this through the short breath meditations at the end of the first three chapters.

To summarize: You inhale deeply, then exhale with a sound. This sound can be as soft as a whisper or as loud as a shout. Whatever it is, just let it be. After inhaling and exhaling in this way several times, you begin to breathe normally. You'll watch the in-breath and the out-breath for several minutes, noticing the subtle expansion and contraction of your body. Your mind will become quieter and your breath will deepen. Then you will be ready to begin the core meditation.

How Do You Use the Meditations in This Book?

In the next section, "The Core Meditations," I will teach you thirteen meditations. They all have been done by meditators with great success.

You will begin with focused meditation. The focused meditations I teach here are simple and easy to do, and most people appreciate their connection to the Jewish tradition.

The first focused meditation, the *hineini* meditation, is the starting point. You should read it carefully, then practice it for several weeks. Even if it doesn't resonate with you right away, stick with it if you can. Soon you'll discover its beauty.

If the *hineini* meditation doesn't feel comfortable for whatever reason, pick another focused meditation and do it instead for several weeks. Solidify your beginning practice by practicing a single meditation rather than jumping around. You'll find that you will be less confused and more successful in your practice this way.

After you have done the *hineini* meditation for at least a month, you will be ready to try the other focused meditations. Pick one that appeals to you, and practice it for a few days. If you like it, keep on with it. If you don't, go to another meditation.

Once you have explored the focused meditations, you can move to the awareness meditations. And finally you can try the emptiness meditations.

Take your time. Don't feel that you have to do all the meditations. The point is to get something out of your practice rather than to know how to do a lot of different meditations. If you end up staying with the *hineini* meditation for the rest of your life, that is fine. There is no reason to move on.

The core meditations are included so that you can experience different possibilities. Most people end up practicing a favorite few and don't deviate very often.

How Do You Prepare to Meditate?

Imagine that you have set up your meditation cushion or chair, and you are now ready to begin your practice. What do you actually do? You meditate, right? Wrong. It's a mistake to jump abruptly from everyday life into meditation. Instead, we move slowly and with care.

You must be absolutely clear about which meditation you are going to do and how you are going to do it. This is the first preparation. If you don't have a meditation in mind, consult the section on core meditations in this book and select one. Read it carefully, absorbing the details of how it is done. Keep the book nearby so that you can refer to it if necessary.

Meditators are often unaware of the importance of this preparation. If you don't know what you are going to do beforehand, your meditation will suffer. You'll fumble around, reviewing the various possibilities in your mind, trying to figure out which one you should choose. This only leads to frustration. So take your time deciding how to spend the next ten minutes. Once you've done this, you are ready to move on.

A second preparation involves readying your body. Take a few minutes to stretch in a way that feels good. It doesn't matter if you are sitting or standing. Some people like to do yoga movements at this time.

Our bodies are tight and tense in certain places, and we don't attend to them enough. As you stretch, become aware of your breath. This is your opportunity to breathe deeply and release the tension you carry.

When you have finished, sit in your chair or on your cushion, making sure that you are comfortable. Shift around until you feel satisfied with your position.

Close your eyes or rest your eyes on a quiet surface such as the carpet or a blank wall. You will focus on your breath for a few minutes, then begin the core meditation.

How Do You Conclude Your Core Meditation?

Take a few deep breaths and slowly open your eyes. If you wish, you can say, "Amen."

Blink your eyes a few times and look around the room.

Become aware of your body on the chair or cushion. Notice how it holds you.

When you are ready, you can begin to move. You might feel like stretching or yawning.

If you need to leave your meditation space right away, rise slowly. When you are standing, feel the floor or ground under your feet.

If you don't need to leave, you might want to reflect on your meditation experience. Or read something that inspires you. Or study something that has special meaning to you.

Whatever you do, realize that it will take several minutes or more before you will be ready to resume your regular activities. You can return to work, but you might not feel like immediately joining in conversation or rushing to meet a deadline.

The effects of meditation linger. If possible, take the time to savor them. You might feel sad about leaving behind the quietness of your practice, but remember, you will be returning to it again tomorrow.

Meditation is like a dance. Its grace is more than the individual movements, but the movements must be made to create its grace. When you first begin your practice, you will feel awkward and unsure of yourself. But it won't take long for your practice to become smooth. As you become familiar with all the details, you'll move seamlessly from preparation to breath, from breath to your meditation, then from your meditation to the ending. Like a dancer, your meditation will flow.

Outline of Meditation from Beginning to End

Preparation

- Decide on your core meditation.
- Prepare your body by stretching.
- Sit comfortably and close your eyes.

Meditation

- Take several deep breaths, making a sound with each exhalation.
- Breathe normally. Observe your breath for a few minutes as your mind quiets down.
- Begin the core meditation.

Conclusion

- Take a few deep breaths, open your eyes.
- Look around the room.
- Rise slowly.

Part Two

The Core Meditations

6

Focused Meditations

Hineini Meditation— Becoming More Fully Present

The Hebrew word *hineini* (pronounced "he-nay-nee") means "Here I am." This word is the focus of your first meditation.

Most of us have difficulty being "here." Our minds jump into the past or the future, and we ignore the present moment. Because of this mental habit, we often feel spiritually depleted and discouraged. We grasp for "highs," failing to understand that we first must cultivate our ability to pay attention in the present moment and deepen our awareness of what we spiritually receive.

My first experience with the *hineini* meditation took place many years ago during a four-day silent retreat with a group of students. After listening to a teaching about the importance of paying attention, we meditated together, focusing on the word *hineini*. Immediately I found it to be a powerful pathway to spiritual experience.

That day, I focused on being "here" by observing my

bodily sensations and silently saying *hineini* over and over again. Whenever my mind wandered, I brought it back to the word. After a while I became one with it so that I didn't need to repeat it as often. And then I became suspended in time and space in the most beautiful way, and experienced the presence of great holiness. My individual self diminished so that I was no longer a separate being. Afterwards, I felt renewed—and more aware of the spiritual dimension of every moment.

Since then I've practiced this meditation regularly. I usually don't have such intense experiences as I did that first time. When I am agitated, my mind wanders and I have difficulty staying with the word *hineini.* But even then, I've found that the meditation helps me become more spiritually aware.

Over the years, I've taught *hineini* to hundreds of students with good results. I encourage you to do it every day for at least a month before you attempt any others. Each time your experience will be different, as *hineini* has an unlimited number of manifestations. Let yourself begin to discover what they are for you.

If you wish, you can continue to practice *hineini* indefinitely. Many students consider this to be their central meditation, the one they return to again and again. Even though they learn other meditations, they prefer it above the rest.

The word *hineini* is potent with meaning in the Jewish tradition. Within the Torah it is most often used to describe a state of utter readiness. The book of Exodus, for example, tells us that the shepherd Moses heard the voice of God speaking to him from a burning bush. "Moses, Moses," God called. *"Hineini,"* he replied. "Here I am" (Exodus 3:4).

Moses' answer conveys his willingness to receive what

will come next. He is physically present, emotionally ready, and spiritually open to the Divine.

Hineini is a centered state of being. It means being "here" in body, mind, and spirit. It means being open to the possibility of spiritual connection.

Hineini is passive in the moment, but alert to the possibility of action in the future, once the meditation is finished.

Hineini is an enormous "Yes!"

The word *hineini* also appears many times in Jewish liturgy in a slightly different form, *hineni*. In the *Hineni* Yom Kippur prayer, for instance, the cantor expresses sorrow for the sins that have taken place in the past year, and pleads for mercy: "Here I am, deficient in good deeds, overcome by awe, and trembling."

Thus, *hineini* also conveys the idea of being present in the most honest, humble way. Rather than inflating the self to hide our flaws, we offer ourselves fully. We know who we are and what we have done. Yet this does not cause us to waver: We still say *hineini*.

The *kavvanah* (holy intention) of the *hineini* meditation is to become more fully present.

Begin by taking a deep breath. As you exhale, make a sound—as you learned to do in the earlier chapters of the book. Do this several times, then settle into your ordinary breathing.

Now watch your breath: Notice how your chest expands and contracts, and how your body receives the breath and lets it go. As you do this, your mind will begin to quiet down and you will start to relax.

When you are ready, move your attention to the word *hineini,* or, if you wish, to the words "Here I am."

Hineini. Here I am.

Focus on *hineini.*
Repeat it silently to yourself.

Hineini. Here I am.

Let the word become filled with your breath.
Merge with it, so that you experience being fully present.

Hineini. Here I am.
Not thinking
Not accomplishing
Not doing
Just being.

Hineini. Here I am.
Full presence
Readiness to receive
In body
Heart
Mind
Spirit

Hineini. Here I am.

When your mind wanders, as it inevitably will, do not judge yourself. Simply notice where it has gone and return to *hineini.*

If you are distracted by the sounds
around you, notice them and
return to *hineini.*

Hineini. Here I am.

Shalom Meditation— Letting in Divine Peace

One of the translations for the Hebrew word *shalom* is "peace." Most of us yearn for peace. At times our minds are burdened, our hearts broken, and our spirits deflated. We want to feel at peace, but this state seems so far away.

The *shalom* meditation is one of the first ones I teach to beginning meditators. The word itself is familiar to everyone, and non-Hebrew-speaking students immediately feel comfortable with it. The image of peace is one they appreciate, and they like being immersed in a deeper state of resolution and acceptance.

We've all seen the word *shalom* printed gaily on greeting cards or posters, and heard it bantered about lightly in conversation. But through meditation, we discover its depths. It is a beautiful word. The *sh* at the beginning and the *om* at the end feel like holy sounds as they reverberate through us.

Indeed, the Hebrew letters in this word are considered to be among the most essential. We find them in other important words. For example, we find the *sh* and the *m* in *Sh'ma,* the first word of the central prayer of the Jewish faith.

The word *shalom* appears in significant places in Jewish liturgy—for example, in the *Kaddish.* And, at the very end of the *Amidah,* the prayer that is considered to be the spiritual highpoint of all services, we find a special prayer for peace:

"May the One Who makes peace in the highest places, make peace for all of us and for all of Israel, and for the whole world, and let us say, Amen."

One of my favorite places where *shalom* appears is in *Ma'ariv,* the evening prayer service. In a blessing after the *Sh'ma,* we say, "Help us, our God, to lie down in peace, and awaken us to life again. Spread over us the shelter of Your peace, and direct us to better ourselves through Your wise counsel." In this prayer we ask for the peace that can come through sleep, knowing that another day will follow, bringing challenges that we hope to face with greater wisdom.

The *kavvanah* of the *shalom* meditation is to open yourself to peace that comes from the Divine.

Settle yourself comfortably, then take a deep breath. As you exhale, make a sound. Do this several times, then resume your normal breathing.

Simply observe your breath. Notice it filling you, then leaving you. Be aware of its rhythmic quality.

Let your mind begin to settle down and your body relax.

Now, shift your attention to *shalom.*
Say the word several times to yourself:

Shalom
Shaaaa . . . lommmm.

With each breath,
feel yourself enveloped in *shalom.*
A peace that holds you,
That protects you,
That gives you strength.

Peace of the Holy One
Holy Peace
Shalom.

When your mind wanders, bring it
back to *shalom.*
If you become distracted, come back
to *shalom.*

Shalom
A shelter of peace for each of us
A safe place
A comforting place
A secure place
that restores us for the hours and
days ahead.

Shalom
Divine Peace
A blessing
Shalom

Divine Light Meditation—Receiving Divine Light

In this meditation we focus on the light of the Divine. With each breath we receive it and experience its presence, using the same meditative technique found in other focused meditations.

You can relate to this meditation in a literal way or a metaphorical way. Some of you will have no difficulty envisioning God as light; others will be more comfortable thinking of light as creative or healing energy, holy in its own way.

Through the centuries Jewish mystics devised many meditations on Divine light. They saw light as a manifestation of God, and especially liked to contemplate its different qualities. At times they stared at burning candles or performed various eye movements to see the spectrum of its colors.

The Divine light meditation is a contemporary meditation, but it parallels many found in the Jewish mystical tradition. It is often used with beginning students because it helps them have an immediate spiritual connection with the Divine. We teach that God as Divine light infuses the universe and is available to everyone. Like the air we breath, it is everywhere—even in a darkened room—but we are usually unaware of its presence.

The imagery of Divine light is found throughout Judaism. In the Torah we read that God's first act, after creating heaven and earth, was to create light: "And God said, 'Let there be light.' And there was light" (Genesis 1:3).

The understanding of God as creator of light is present also within the liturgy. In one of the blessings before the *Sh'ma* in the morning service, we praise God for bringing on the morning light after the dark of night, and we end with, "Blessed is *Adonai,* Creator of light(s)."

The connection between God and light goes even further. Not only does God *create* light, but God *is* light. Light radiates outward, through the universe, in a multitude of hues. Toward the end of the *Amidah* in the prayer book, we find the phrase, "Bless us, our God, with the light of Your presence."

Isaac Luria, the sixteenth-century Kabbalist, spoke about the beginning of existence when the entire universe was God as Divine essence. God then contracted to make room for creation to take place. Divine light emanated through the space that was opened, and it is still present today for all of us to receive.

The *kavvanah* of the Divine light meditation is to open yourself to the light of the Divine.

Once you have settled on your cushion or chair, take several slow, deep breaths. Make a sound with each exhalation, letting go of the pressures of the day.

Now begin to breathe regularly.
Breath in.
Breath out.

With each inhalation, receive the light
of the Divine.
Experience its beauty and boundless
strength.
Its color
Its warmth
Its radiance
Its cascading creative energy.

With each breath in, the light of the
Divine fills you.

It gives you a feeling of well-being
Clarity
Strength.

With each exhalation, the light of the
Divine passes through you.
Healing you
Cleansing you
Releasing the toxins of your everyday
life.

With each in-breath, receiving the
presence of Divine light.
With each out-breath, experiencing the
gift of Divine light.

When your thoughts wander, as they
inevitably will, gently encircle
them with light and return to the
focus of the meditation.

Breath in.
Breath out.

If you become distracted by a sound
or a movement around you,
notice it, then return to the focus of
the meditation.

Divine light.
God's presence.

Chesed Meditation—Opening Your Heart

Chesed (pronounced "hes-sed")is a Hebrew word that means "loving-kindness." For us to have *chesed,* our hearts must be opened.

Who among us has a really open heart? Anger, frustration, and fear accumulate in our everyday lives, and we become self-protective. A certain hardness settles over us without our noticing it, and we turn away from others. This state of alienation can be intensely experienced, as when we are in the heat of an argument. Or it can go on indefinitely in a chronic way, becoming dominant in our personality.

When we open our hearts, we are able to love in a more unconditional way. Our response to others comes from *chesed,* not from anger or fear. Some people mistakenly think that *chesed* can cause us to become manipulated by others' desires and demands. But we can wisely balance love with an awareness of our own needs so that we don't give away too much of ourselves and become depleted.

The *chesed* meditation can be extremely useful in breaking through the barriers around the heart. Students who carry a lot of anger find it especially helpful, and I encourage them to take it on as a regular practice.

This meditation might remind you of Buddhist *metta* (loving-kindness) practice. It differs, however, because we frame what we are doing in a Jewish context, with teachings about love that exist within our tradition.

In Judaism we hold the understanding that God loves the people Israel and all humankind. This love is revealed by God's acts of compassion and kindness toward us. One of the psalms, for example, describes the relationship this way: "Adonai is my shepherd, I shall not want. Adonai makes me lie down in lush pastures and leads me beside tranquil waters. Adonai restores my soul, and guides me in the paths of righteousness. Though I walk in the valley of the shadow of death, I will fear no evil for You are with me, Your rod and Your staff, they comfort me" (Psalm 23:1–4).

This intense love between God and us is also expressed in The Song of Songs, a love poem between a man and a woman that is often interpreted as a metaphor for the love of God for Israel: "My beloved is mine and I am his" (Song of Songs 6:3). God is so intimately intertwined with human beings that we don't know which is the beloved and which is the speaker.

One of the most beautiful prayers in *Shacharit,* the morning prayer service, expresses the love of God: *Ahavah raba Ahavtanu,* "With a great love, God has loved us." This love is a gift, one that is unconditionally given and received.

At the same time that we are loved, we are also instructed to love the Divine: "And you shall love the Lord your God with all your heart, and all your soul, and all your might" (Deuteronomy 6:5). This outpouring of love on our part is our response to the Divine love we have received.

In Jewish mysticism we are taught that love is part of ongoing creation. It emanates from and exists within the Divine, and is available to us. We don't manufacture love ourselves; it already exists. Thus we don't have to feel the strain of creating it anew. Instead, we enter into the stream of love by opening our hearts so that we receive it, and it radiates through us to others.

The *kavvanah* of the *chesed* meditation is to open your heart so that you more easily experience love.

Take several deep breaths as usual, making a sound with your exhalation. Then settle into your regular breathing.

When you are ready to begin, focus on opening your heart.

As you inhale, let your heart soften.
Receiving love
From God
From those close to you
Even from strangers.

Those unexpected moments, so large
and so small,
when you receive this gift.

As you exhale, let the love pass
through you
And beyond,
To those you already love
To those you hardly know
To those with whom you are angry.
And to strangers.

When your mind wanders, notice
where it has gone, and return to
the focus.
When you become distracted, bring
your attention back to *chesed.*

Breath in, receiving love.
Breath out, radiating love.

Chesed, loving kindness.
There for all of us
No matter who we are.
No matter what we do.

Thankfulness Meditation— Filling with Gratitude

The Hebrew words for "I am thankful" are *modah ani* (pronounced "mo-dah ah-nee") for women, and *modeh ani* ("mo-day ah-nee") for men.

Often we don't notice the blessings in our lives. Our attention goes to those things that are missing rather than those that are present. The feeling of desire keeps us unsettled and preoccupied, and leads us to search frantically for more love, more honor, more material possessions.

In this meditation we focus entirely on what we receive. When we become aware of what already exists in our lives, we discover that the list is longer than we realized. Even if we haven't found the partner of our dreams, or we're feeling ill, or we've suffered a great loss, there are always blessings. The kind look of the stranger in the store yesterday, or the whiteness of the clouds overhead today, can be a good beginning.

I especially like to practice this meditation early in the morning. When I am aware of the gifts in my life, it helps me take on the responsibilities of the day in a more gracious way.

At the meditation center where I teach, we often do a thankfulness meditation by having people focus on *modah ani* or *modeh ani,* the Hebrew words for "I am thankful." I've found that this meditation is especially useful for those who carry a great deal of negativity or dissatisfaction. At first they are afraid they won't be able to do it. But once they start, they are surprised by the abundance of blessings they receive.

The expression of gratitude is one of the most important

parts of Jewish liturgy. Observant Jews, for example, say the following prayer upon rising: "I am thankful to You, living and everlasting King, for You have restored my soul with mercy." Gratitude is integrated into all three daily prayer services. God is seen as the One Who gives us abundance and fills our lives with favor. Acknowledging this aspect of Divine nature is considered to be extremely important.

Traditional Jews typically declare their gratitude by saying a blessing whenever anything good happens. This includes the familiar blessing over food, but also a blessing on seeing an old friend, or wearing a new piece of clothing, or even going to the toilet first thing in the morning. As one rabbinic statement directs, "Whosoever partakes of the goodness of the world without acknowledging its source is a thief!"

The tradition teaches us the importance of remaining conscious of all that we receive from God. In the Talmud Jews are told to say one hundred blessings a day. Even if we are not traditional Jews, and even if our God-consciousness is different from that expressed above, this is a good practice.

We learn that we don't have to manufacture gratitude or use our will to create it. Instead, we open ourselves to the Divine stream of blessings and become part of the flow. Over time this gratitude becomes an integral part of our daily lives.

The *kavvanah* of the thankfulness meditation is to become filled with gratitude.

Take several full breaths, releasing a sound with your exhalation. Then begin to breathe in your normal way. Observe the breath for a few minutes until you are ready to begin.

Now focus on the words *modeh ani*
(for men)
or *modah ani* (for women),
or on the words "I am thankful."

Silently say the words over and over.
Hear them in your mind's ear.
Feel them resonate within you.

Or visualize the words.
Trace them in your mind's eye.
See them carved out against a colored
background.

Merge with the words.
Become one with thankfulness.
Let it fill you.

Invite the images of gratitude to
appear.
The people
The experiences
The opportunities
The minutes
The nanoseconds.

Name them.
Dwell on them.

Modah ani.
Modeh ani.
I am thankful.

With your breath, feel your gratitude
Breath in, receiving these gifts.
Breath out, returning your gratitude.

When your mind wanders, bring it
back to thankfulness.
When you are distracted, return to the
focus.

Modeh ani.
Modah ani.
I am thankful.

No gift is too large
No gift is too small
For gratitude.

Neshamah Meditation—Experiencing Your Soul Within

One of the Hebrew words for soul is *neshamah* (pronounced "neh-shah-mah"). The concept of soul is confusing for many of us. We can't locate our soul anywhere in our bodies nor can we point to its existence, so we wonder if it is real.

Yet we sense that there is something within us that is "pure" or uncontaminated. Despite our imperfections, despite all the times we've done harm, we know in our most reasonable moments that we're not entirely bad. Even the most destructive people throughout history have a core of goodness, although it is buried beneath their evil acts and exists only in potential form.

I like to lead students in a simple meditation that focuses on the words, *Elohai, neshamah shenatata be, t'horah he* (pronounced "el-oh-high, neh-shah-mah sh-nah-tah-tah bee, tay-hor-ah hee"). Or in English, "My God, the soul You have given me is pure." Those who are comfortable with Hebrew can use the Hebrew words, but it works just as well in English.

This meditation is especially helpful for people who have lost sight of their own goodness and who dwell on their imperfections. Once they experience the soul within as an undeniable reality, they more easily let go of the self-inflated idea of their own insignificance.

The words for this meditation come from the early part of the morning service. The prayer says, "My God, the soul You have given me is pure. You formed it, You breathed it into me, and You preserve it within me. You will take my soul from me, but You will restore it in the time to come." Thus we see soul as hosted by us, but not owned by us. We do not create it, because it already exists.

According to the Jewish mystical tradition five aspects of soul dwell within each of us. They are related to each other, but have different characteristics. The first of these, *nefesh,* is the soul that is given to us at birth and that leaves us when we die. It's the most tangible, earthly aspect of soul. Next comes *ruach,* which exists on the level of deep understanding. It's that part within us that makes intuitive leaps. The third aspect of soul is *neshamah.* Here we find the spark of the Divine revealed most strongly. The final two aspects are beyond anything we can know or sense, because they are so much a part of the Divine. Thus they are hardly mentioned.

Soul exists in all of us, but it is bound and hidden by our negative traits. For some people it is hardly present. But as we do our self-refinement and take responsibility for our self-destructive, harmful ways, the soul within us becomes more and more revealed. Over time, then, we become more "soulful," and able to relate to others and to God in deeper ways.

The *kavvanah* of the *neshamah* meditation is to experience the soul within.

Make yourself comfortable, then breathe deeply, making a sound with your exhalation. Do this several times, letting go of the tension within you.

Let your breath settle into its usual rhythm.

Observe it for a few minutes.

When your mind has quieted down, you are ready to begin.

Focus on the words, "My God, the soul
 You have given me is pure."
Or *Elohai, neshamah shenatata be,*
 t'horah he.

Say the words silently to yourself over
 and over.
Say them with each breath.

With each breath, receive the soul.
Experience the soul.
Know the soul.

Feel the connection with God,
The source of soul
The provider of soul.

If your mind wanders, observe where
it went and bring it back to the
meditation.

If a noise or movement distracts you,
let it go.

"My God, the soul You have given me
is pure."
Elohai, neshamah shenatata be,
t'horah he.

Sh'ma Meditation—Merging with the Sounds of the *Sh'ma*

The *Sh'ma,* a well-known prayer central to Jewish faith, is said as follows: "*Sh'ma Yisrael, Adonai Eloheinu, Adonai Ehad*" (pronounced "sh-ma yis-rah-el, ah-doe-nahy el-o-hay-nu, ah-doe-nahy eh-hahd). This prayer is often translated as "Listen, Israel. Adonai is our God. Adonai is One."

Perhaps you've heard stories about people repeating the *Sh'ma* as they approach death. Or maybe you were taught as a child to whisper it before going to sleep. Or you say it regularly as a part of Jewish liturgy. Whatever your connection to it, you probably resonate with its words on many levels.

I first learned the *Sh'ma* meditation several years ago from a teacher who brought it to the United States from Israel. It has been transmitted down through the centuries, although its exact origin is unknown.

At our meditation center many people appreciate this meditation because they say it helps them learn to concentrate better than any other meditation. When they are filled with the sound of these holy words, all other thoughts disappear.

In this meditation the breath and the words of the *Sh'ma* are put together. You might want to practice it before you actually do it as a meditation, because it takes a few moments to learn. The meditation begins by silently saying the first two words, *Sh'ma Yisrael,* while inhaling. Then you'll say *Adonai Eloheinu* while exhaling. Then *Adonai Ehad* while inhaling. It begins all over again, with the first two words said silently while exhaling. As you'll see, the first phrase of the prayer alternates between the inhalation and the exhalation.

In traditional Judaism the *Sh'ma* is spoken only at certain prescribed times. Its significance is so great that it is prohibited to say it lightly. But in this meditation the *Sh'ma* is repeated silently and respectfully; therefore, it is considered acceptable.

The *Sh'ma* can be seen as a simple declaration of belief in one God: "Listen everyone, pay attention! God is our God. God is One Being." This declaration seems to say that God is outside of us, the patriarchal Father-in-the-Sky, the God of Jewish history, and that we should acknowledge that this is the only God.

But Jewish mysticism opens up the understanding of God to include God as Immanent Being, present in all life. The Holy Sparks exist within vessels as small as a tiny insect or a blade of grass.

If God exists in all life, then we humans are part of God. The Oneness of God includes us too.

Thus the *Sh'ma* can be seen as a call to become aware of that spark of divinity within ourselves. To nourish it. To help it expand.

And it is a call to honor the presence of holiness in all living beings, because they too are part of God. And it is a call to see the connection, the Oneness, of us all.

The *kavvanah* of the *Sh'ma* meditation is to merge with the sound of the words of the *Sh'ma.*

Take several full, deep breaths, letting out a sound with each exhalation.

Begin to breath normally.
Observe the gentle rise and fall of
your breath.
The sound of it entering
The sound of it leaving.

When you are ready, silently repeat
the words of the *Sh'ma.*

Breath in: *Sh'ma Yisrael*
Breath out: *Adonai Eloheinu*
Breath in: *Adonai Ehad.*

Then immediately begin again.

Breath out: *Sh'ma Yisrael*
Breath in: *Adonai Eloheinu*
Breath out: *Adonai Ehad.*

Focus all your attention on the sound
of these words.
Don't think about them.
Don't analyze them.
Don't try to figure out their meaning.

Simply let the sound of the words fill
you.
Let it reverberate through you.
Receive it.
Hear it.
Listen.

Sh'ma Yisrael, Adonai Eloheinu,
Adonai Ehad.

If you become distracted, begin the
Sh'ma again.
If your mind wanders, notice where it
went and bring it back to the
Sh'ma.

Let yourself become enveloped in the
sound of these holy words.
Sh'ma Yisrael
Adonai Eloheinu
Adonai Ehad.

Yod-Hay-Vav-Hay Meditation—Focusing on the Letters of God's Name

The unpronounceable name of the Divine is spelled with the Hebrew letters *yod-hay-vav-hay*. You can see this word, written in Hebrew from right to left, on page 107.

The word is visually beautiful. Many of the lines are parallel, and the repeated letter *hay* gives the shape balance and stability. Even if you don't know Hebrew, you can absorb the power of the word by gazing at it.

In Jewish mysticism Hebrew letters are considered to be

more than just letters: They hold the essence of the universe. When they are put together, they create words that have mystical implications beyond the defined meaning of the word.

When we meditate with letters, as with this *yod-hay-vav-hay* meditation, we can sense or experience these deeper meanings, without being told. They are there in front of us, if we are open.

The *yod-hay-vav-hay* meditation differs from others that we have done before. Rather than focusing on a sound, an image, or our breath, we look at these letters, either on paper or in our mind's eye. Thus we focus visually on the Divine Name.

I first learned this meditation from a rabbi who has a longstanding Zen Buddhist meditation practice. Sometimes he brings this meditation into it, focusing all his attention on the letters of the Divine Name. This meditation goes back many centuries: Kabbalistic meditators often practiced it, using various forms. Today, many people say they appreciate the technique of contemplating letters because it helps them experience the Divine Name in new ways.

Judaism holds the belief that the Divine is ultimately indefinable. We humans cannot even begin to know who or what God is. The best we can do is name what we experience, acknowledging that the Holy is beyond comprehension.

Through history many Hebrew names for God have been devised. Each one reflects a different dimension of Divine Being as we see it. Thus we have *Adonai* as sovereign being and mighty power, *Elohim* as judge, and *Shekhinah* as the indwelling One who sustains and nourishes us. There are also the androgynous names of *Yah* (High One), and *HaMakom* (The Holy Place).

We hold these God-names close to us, running our tongues over them, creating images of God from the sounds.

But we can't do this with the name *yod-hay-vav-hay.* We can't even pronounce it.

This name is considered to be higher and more true than the others. It is sight without sound, part revealed and part unrevealed. Thus we gaze at the letters and absorb them, but we are not given the sounds, except as we experience them in the silence within.

The *kavvanah* of the *yod-hay-vav-hay* meditation is to visually merge with the letters.

Before you begin, read through the meditation then put the book in front of you, opened to page 107.

Take several deep breaths, exhaling with whatever sound is within you.

Resume your normal breathing. Pay close attention to it as your mind begins to settle down and your body relaxes.

When you are ready, gaze at the
Divine name on the page. Or close
your eyes and see the letters in
your mind's eye.

Observe the shape of each letter.
Its height
Its breadth.
See the lines of the letters meeting.
See the lines of the letters diverging.

Notice how the letters fit together.
Their closeness
Their distance.

Continue with this meditation. At any time, you can close your eyes and trace the letters in your mind's eye.

Yod
Hay
Vav
Hay

Say the letters silently to yourself.
Yod Hay Vav Hay

Open to their beauty.
Explore their spaciousness.
Let them enter you.
Let yourself enter them.

This is the Divine Name of God.
The Mystery of Being
The Presence
The Name.

יהוה

Hebrew Letters for the *Yod-Hay-Vav-Hay* Meditation
(Written from Right to Left)

Hebrew calligraphy from *The Book of Letters* by Lawrence Kushner.
Woodstock, Vt.: Jewish Lights Publishing, 1990.

7
Awareness Meditations

Gam Zeh Kadosh Meditation—Becoming Aware of the Workings of the Mind

Gam zeh kadosh (pronounced "gaum zeh ka-dosh") means "This, too, is holy."

During meditation we often fall into the habit of judging our thoughts rather than letting them rise and fall without measure. We become so engrossed in this enterprise that we lose sight of what we are doing. Then we suffer because our meditation gets bogged down with self-consciousness and analysis.

The *gam zeh kadosh* meditation helps us stop this habit. Sitting silently, we allow our thoughts to emerge as they will. When we notice what we are thinking, we name it, and then we say to ourselves, "This, too, is holy," or "*Gam zeh kadosh.*" With this blessing, the thought usually dissipates and another soon emerges.

The intention of the meditation is to become more aware of the workings of the mind and to experience the impermanence of thought. The meditation differs from a focused meditation in that we don't focus on a single point. A great deal of concentration is required to observe and name what goes through our minds. And it takes courage to accept all of our thoughts without blame or censure.

In the end, we experience our thoughts as transitory. We cannot grab hold of them: They are like water washing over us. The all-important "I" recedes, and we become part of the larger cosmos.

Students should ground themselves in focused meditation before beginning awareness meditation. Although this latter form of meditation appears to be easy, many people find it more difficult to meditate without a focus. They'd rather be filled with an image, word, or sound than spend the time in the presence of their own thoughts. Still, this practice is useful because it develops awareness.

Jewish awareness meditation resembles Buddhist mindfulness practice. The process of observing the mind is the same. However, we put the meditation in a Jewish context by including the blessing *gam zeh kadosh.* In this way, a connection is made between our thoughts and the Holy Presence in all being.

This meditation has evolved in my own practice over a period of several years. I was familiar with Buddhist mindfulness practice and saw its value in increasing awareness. But I wanted to expand it to include the Jewish understanding that our thoughts are holy in and of themselves. At first, I used *gam zeh tov* ("This, too, is good"), then changed it to its present form.

In the eighteenth and nineteenth centuries Hasidic rabbis taught that the thoughts that go through our minds during meditation are there for a reason. We have something to learn from them. Therefore they should not be rejected, even if their content seems insignificant or negative.

These thoughts are important material for the self-refinement that each of us is doing. If I habitually have angry, envious, or judgmental thoughts during meditation, this is a good indication that I have some work to do in these areas. Through noticing these thoughts, then, I can face the tasks ahead. I can begin to cultivate more wholesome thoughts that will help to transform my heart.

The Hasidic mystics took the acceptance of the mind's workings even further. They said that because God is present in all life, every thought contains a spark of holiness. During meditation, the Divine exists in the workings of our minds, and should be remembered at all times. Negative thoughts are energy that has gone in undesirable directions. We acknowledge the source of this energy, and we work to rectify those thoughts.

The *kavvanah* of the *gam zeh kadosh* meditation is to become aware of the workings of the mind.

Begin by taking several deep breaths. Make a sound each time you exhale, letting go of the tension within you.

Now breathe normally.
Observe your breath for a few
moments:
Its gentle rise and fall
Its rhythm.

When you are ready, let go of your
breath observation.
Sit silently, watching your thoughts as
they emerge.

Let your mind wander.
Don't restrain it.
One thought, then another.

When you notice where your mind has gone, name it silently:
I'm worrying about my job.
I'm obsessing about what my partner said today.
I'm judging my friend.
I'm planning how I'll get the car fixed.
I'm rehearsing what I will say in class tomorrow.
I'm aware that my heart is open.
I'm noticing that I feel content and peaceful.

After you have named your thought,
Give it your blessing.
Gam zeh kadosh.
This, too, is holy.

One thought cresting like a wave,
then receding:
Gam zeh kadosh.

And then another:
This, too, is holy.

And another.

Walking Meditation—Increasing Awareness of the World Around us

We move through our lives without paying attention to what is around us. This habit is useful because we couldn't function if we responded to every sensory stimulus. But our field of vision decreases without our awareness, and we fail to notice the narrowness of our vision.

A walking meditation can help us increase our sensitivity to that which is outside ourselves. At first, this kind of meditation might seem labored and strange, but as we learn to open our senses more fully and see the lines, shapes, colors, and objects within our view, we gain a broader appreciation of the wondrous world in which we live.

The goal of this walking meditation is to become more conscious of this world. Meditators walk in a slow, deliberate way with their eyes open, looking carefully at whatever comes into their sight.

We teach this meditation in a Jewish context, with the understanding that all matter—living or not—is infused with holiness. In the *gam zeh kadosh* awareness meditation we blessed each thought and accepted it as holy. In this walking meditation we continue that approach to everything we see: All matter contains the spark of God, and we acknowledge this as we slowly walk.

I first did this meditation in a beautiful retreat center on the California coast. During a weekend of silence, the meditators alternated the *hineini* sitting meditation with a walking meditation. We sat for forty minutes, then walked for ten minutes, then sat, then walked again. As the hours passed, the light in the room became more diffuse and everything looked softer. A high moment for me was walking meditatively in front of the huge windows as the sun set slowly over the Pacific Ocean.

I often practice this walking meditation by myself because it helps me become conscious of the glory that surrounds me. On warm days I like to do it in my garden. Like everyone else, I filter what comes into my view. But when I see—*really* see—I am enlivened and inspired.

This meditation is especially good for those who feel stale, bored, or diminished in vigor. They have become so accustomed to the blinders on their spiritual vision that they don't even know the possibilities that exist. Once their vision begins to open, they feel themselves expand with appreciation.

The Torah begins with Genesis and the familiar story of creation: "In the beginning God created the heaven and the earth." It goes on to include the introduction of darkness and light, water and land, vegetation, living creatures of all kinds, and human beings.

We are told that everything that existed in the beginning was created by God, from the smallest insect to the towering mountains. Even though we might not accept the biblical account of creation as literally true, we understand that the Divine is central to all existence.

God created the universe—but God did not stop. The world is created anew every moment. We see this most obviously in the growth of a baby, or the budding of a rose, but all around us, and within us, change continues. Since God is present in the unfolding of creation, every object is infused with holiness.

Jewish mysticism, as we've already said, teaches us that all matter holds the living sparks of the Divine. We approach everything outside ourselves as Holy. We walk through this world of impermanence, where everything is being created anew, with respect and reverence.

The *kavvanah* of the walking meditation is to increase our awareness of the world around us.

Before beginning this meditation, find a place where you can move slowly. An outside area is especially good. Visually chart your path so that you know where you are going, and check to make sure there are no obstacles.

Once you know what you are doing, stand at your starting point. If you are disabled, move your wheelchair there. Take several deep breaths. As usual, let out a sound upon exhalation.

> Now breathe normally. Feel your breath enter and leave. Notice your body receiving it and letting it go. Keep your eyes open as you do this, and look around you.
>
> When you are ready, begin to move in very slow motion along your path. A good way to do this is to let your heel touch the ground first, then roll onto the ball of your foot as the other heel is raised and comes down. Do this as slowly as you can, without causing discomfort or imbalance. If you are in a wheelchair, move very slowly along your path.
>
> Look carefully around you as you move.
> Notice the objects:
> Their textures
> Their lines

Their shapes
Their colors.

Each object, shimmering with
holiness.
God in all creation
Unfolding.

If you stop paying attention and your
mind wanders, slow down.
Fix your gaze on one thing.
Stay with it until it reveals its glory.

Take your time.
When you become distracted,
remember to look carefully.
Name what you see.
Flower blooming,
Rock resting,
Soil generating,
Chair inviting,
White purifying,
Red vibrating,
Edge distinguishing.

Each is a gift of God.
Each is a part of creation unfolding.

8

Emptiness Meditations—Quieting the Mind

Ayin Breath Meditation

Jewish mysticism calls the state of emptiness *ayin* (pronounced "aye-in").

Ordinarily our minds don't stay still for long. They jump between fragments of observations, judgments, formulations, and considerations, and we can't seem to stop this interior clamoring. Often we find ourselves yearning for peace.

At these moments we can quiet our minds by moving into emptiness. This state exists, we know, because we have times when our thoughts move more slowly and we experience the space between them. Through emptiness meditation we learn to enter this spaciousness.

I advise students to first become skilled in focused meditation, then awareness meditation, before trying *ayin* practice. Although longtime meditators have less difficulty with it, beginners usually do not find it effective. For a few, it can even make them feel ungrounded because they are not yet comfortable with the vast silence within.

This *ayin* breath meditation is a favorite among experienced meditators. One student, for example, finds it to be a counterbalance to his tendency to obsess about all those things currently angering him. When he gets to a state beyond thought for even a short time through this meditation, he can let go of anger more easily in his everyday life.

Some people fear that the state of emptiness is the same as death, with darkness all around and a cessation of being. But this is mistaken. It's more like floating in a warm ocean, held up by salt water, surrounded by teeming organic life, the sun and sky overhead—and just being there, without a single thought. Emptiness is filled with creative possibility, only it isn't formed. The mind becomes silent and enters this state, but everything else around us continues to exist.

In *ayin* everything is possible and nothing is happening. It's like that wondrous moment before inhaling, when the lungs are deflated and the breath has not begun to enter. The body is quiet—until you begin to breathe again.

Ayin gives rise to creation. Just as the lungs expand with the breath, emptiness soon becomes filled. But before that happens, *ayin* exists. And that is where emptiness meditation takes place.

The *kavvanah* of *ayin* breath meditation is to quiet our mind and move into a state of emptiness.

Before beginning this meditation, take several deep breaths. Exhale fully, with whatever sound is within you.

Now begin to breathe in your regular
fashion.
Pay careful attention to your
inhalation and your exhalation.
Breath in.
Breath out.

Notice that moment just before the
breath enters your nostrils:
That moment of deflation
That moment of emptiness
That moment of stillness.

Descend into that state.
No-thought
No-thing
This is *ayin.*

Immerse yourself in emptiness.
Be present in *ayin.*

Let your thoughts cease.
Just be.
Be.

When your mind wanders, return to
the moment before breathing.
Ayin.

If you become distracted, return to
emptiness again.
Ayin.

A still, quiet state.
Holding all possibility
But empty
Peaceful.
Ayin.

Space-between-the-Letters Meditation—Entering into Emptiness

In the previous meditation we moved into a state of *ayin* through the breath. This is an easy way to discover how it feels to be immersed in emptiness.

Perhaps you found yourself suspended for moments in this state. Most of us cannot stay there for long, because our minds kick into action. What, no thought? Unthinkable! So a vision or a concern emerges, and we are back on familiar ground.

Often the thoughts that arise during emptiness meditation are creative and insightful, like the thoughts that come in the middle of the night. Or we might have a sense of the presence of God or great holiness. This is because the individual self is in a state of unboundedness, suspended in time and space. The temptation exists to begin to ruminate about the brilliant understanding that suddenly comes to us during the meditation, or to analyze the spiritual moment. But of course, this immediately takes us out of *ayin.*

Significant thoughts or experiences during meditation usually will stay with you. You don't have to stop and write them down, as if they were dreams. You might not remember the details, but they become part of you. Therefore it is important to return right away to *ayin* rather than get caught up with your own process. Do it again and again throughout the meditation, if necessary.

The following meditation comes directly from the

Kabbalistic tradition. When students practice it, they enter into the stream of history and feel close to the generations of mystics in the past. They also appreciate its simplicity.

In Jewish mysticism Hebrew letters are considered to contain the elements of the universe. When we focus on them, as we did with the *yod-hay-vav-hay* focused meditation in chapter 6, we can feel their power.

However, the space around and between letters is just as potent. The space is *ayin,* emptiness—which gives birth to the letters. Mystics in the past used to meditate by carving out the letters in their minds and merging into this empty space.

Judaism is a religion of distinctions. Perhaps you are familiar with some of them: day and night, pure and impure. Each has its functions, but they are not to be subsumed into one. The distinction between letters and space exists in the same way. Thus in our meditation on the space between letters, we push aside the letters and move only into the space.

The *kavvanah* of the space-between-the-letters meditation is to enter into emptiness.

Before you begin, open this book to page 107, where you will see the letters of the Divine Name, *yod-hay-vav-hay.* You can keep the book open for the length of this meditation, or you can close your eyes and visualize the space around these letters in your mind's eye. If you want to refer to the book, put it before you now and prop it open.

Once you have made this arrangement, take several deep breaths. Exhale with a full sound, as usual.

Breathe normally, and observe your
breath for a few minutes until
your mind begins to quiet down.

When you are ready, look at the page,
or close your eyes and visualize
the illustration.

Notice the space around the letters.
Between the letters
Within the letters.

Space holding
Space creating
Space giving birth.

Let yourself merge into this space.
Become one with space.
With emptiness
No-thought
No-thing.

Just be present in the space.
Float in it.
Stay in it.

When your mind wanders, notice
where it has gone and immerse
yourself again in the space.

Emptiness
Ayin.

If you become distracted by noise or
movements around you, notice
your distraction and move back
into the space between the letters.

Emptiness
Ayin.

When the letters intrude on your
consciousness, go between them
or around them. Or push them
aside.

Emptiness
Ayin.

Beyond-the-Self Meditation—Emptying the Self

By now you have discovered through meditation that you are preoccupied with yourself and your concerns. All those hours of sitting have shown you how much time you spend in the "I" state of mind: "I should . . ." "I want . . ." "I consider . . ." "I judge . . ." "I feel . . ."

We're so used to putting ourselves at the center of the universe that we can hardly fathom that there is another way to live. But through the centuries, meditation has helped many people transcend this egocentric view of reality.

Early in this book I introduced the idea of self-refinement. We all need to do it if we are going to become our fullest and most effective selves. It involves working with our anger, pride, guilt, envy, or whatever our core issues are. But for each of us it also means letting go of the image of ourselves as better, worse, or different than others. Of course we are unique beings, but we are not as special as we think. In the grand scheme of things we are very small.

I recommend the following meditation for people who already have a lot of experience with emptiness meditation. It is not easy, but I offer it here because it can be extremely valuable, especially for those with an evaluating, judging, analyzing voice in their minds that keeps them separate and discontent.

The meditation requires repeatedly asking and answering the question "Who is the 'I' who is breathing?" As you will soon see, this mental activity causes the layers of selfhood to fall away and the perception of individuality to disintegrate. Finally, the meditator enters into *ayin,* a state of emptiness.

Jewish mysticism teaches the concept of Divine Oneness: As living beings, we are part of the larger Whole rather than individual entities. We are less permanent than we usually think: The cells in our bodies regenerate every seven years. And eventually, when we turn to dust, we are meant to become part of the ever changing earth.

The "I," then, is only a working construct. We use it in this lifetime, but it binds us. When we get beyond it, we discover the glory of the universe. Without the lens of "I," we finally experience union with all being.

And once we are there, in this larger understanding, we go back into our lives with a more humble sense of self. It doesn't matter so much if we are accepted, or appreciated, or rejected, or scorned, because the self doesn't need to be inflated or defended. It no longer is a fragile and separate ego. Rather, it is part of the larger Whole, and receives sustenance from it.

The *kavvanah* of the beyond-the-self meditation is to empty the self.

Take several full breaths, making a sound of any kind as you exhale.

Now begin to breathe normally.
Notice the way your breath enters
And departs.

Notice your chest swelling
And contracting.

Focus on your breath for a few
minutes.
Now ask yourself this question:
Who is the "I" who is breathing?

Answer your question:
The "I" is . . .

Then ask again:
Who is the "I" who is breathing?

The "I" is . . .

And again:
Who is the "I" who is . . .?

On and on.
Ask the question.
Give your answer.

Layers and layers of selfhood
Revealed

Unmasked
Disintegrated.

Until . . .

You stop.

Emptiness.
Nothing.
No-thing.

The self beyond description
The self merged with Beyond
No more words.

Just presence.

If you start thinking again, go back to the question.
If you become distracted, begin once more.
Who is the "I" who is breathing?

Emptiness.
Ayin.

Part Three

A Meditative Life

9

Challenges of a Meditative Life

By now, many of you have begun to meditate. Even if you aren't doing it as often or as long as you would like, you are experiencing the rewards and the challenges of this practice.

For the next year or so you will remain a beginning meditator. It takes that long for your practice to solidify. In that time you will learn a lot more about the process of meditation and about yourself as a meditator.

One of the things you will discover is that meditation becomes a way of life. The more you meditate, the more you become used to it. When you don't do it, you'll feel unsettled, edgy, or distracted. Something will seem to be missing.

You'll also find that meditation begins to affect the rest of your life. If, for example, you've taken up an exercise such as walking, you know what I mean. Walking can lead to reconsidering your diet, which can lead to reevaluating your health, which can lead to going to a yoga class, which can lead to meeting new people who will walk with you.

Meditation acts in a similar way. You will find yourself doing things that you never expected. You might take a class on spiritual autobiography or read books on Jewish history, subjects that failed to interest you in the past. Or you might decide to study Hebrew, even though you still may feel ambivalent about Judaism.

As meditation becomes integrated into your life, you will be surprised to see old habits shift. One student of mine always used to watch late-night television, but now he finds the noise jarring, so he reads before falling asleep. Another student used to drive fast, always trying to get ahead of other drivers. Now she is slower-paced.

Each meditator is different. The direction of change isn't necessarily toward introversion, as you might think. A long-time meditator friend of mine says that she is more outgoing and involved with people than before. She used to be shy, but now she more readily shows her interest in others. Another is discovering that he has more to contribute during casual conversations because he pays more attention to what is going on around him.

Meditators frequently notice that their values, as well as their habits, shift over time. The sweetness of spiritual experience fills them, and they have less interest in material possessions. Or they treasure their family and friends more than before. Or they become even more committed to helping others. Or they no longer are as interested in pursuing positions of power.

I am not suggesting that Jewish meditation produces instant *tzadikim* (righteous people). Far from it. As long as we are alive, we are all imperfect. We live in this world, not above it. But meditation does have a great impact. At first it is an activity that is inserted into a busy life. Over time, however, the life itself is shaped by meditation.

Meditation can be life-changing, but the practice itself isn't always easy. Many difficulties emerge. Experienced meditators are familiar with them, but they will be new to you. For guidance you can draw from the wisdom accumulated through the years by other meditators.

I like to think of the difficulties we experience in meditation as challenges, not obstacles. They cause us distress, but they help us grow. By working through them we learn important lessons and they refine our understanding of the spiritual path.

Too often we think that transformation comes at the end of many years of meditation. But it is a process that takes place all along the way. With each frustrating moment we have the possibility of learning more.

Probably you won't relish the appearance of these challenges, and you might easily forget their value. But if you can keep in mind that they also provide the opportunity for spiritual transformation, you will not be so overwhelmed when they arise.

Keeping Your Practice Going

The task of maintaining a practice is the most immediate challenge for beginning meditators. In the first section of the book I suggested that you meditate ten minutes each day. I imagine that many of you were not able to do this. Even though your intentions were good, you often got sidetracked by other activities, or you forgot about meditating, or you put it off until the next day or the weekend. This was not a failure on your part: It only points to how hard it is to keep a practice going.

This challenge is more difficult for beginners because the habit of meditation has not yet been formed. As time passes and your practice is integrated into your life, it becomes easier. Still, the challenge never goes away. Even experienced meditators drop off from meditating, and have to begin again.

The practice of meditation takes discipline. There's no way around it. Discipline is easier if you have a routine, however. The purpose of meditating at the same time and in the same place is to reinforce your practice. If you have to decide each day where and when you're meditating, your practice will seem optional—and be more readily dismissed.

If you like to write, you will find it useful to keep a journal about your meditative experience. This will help regularize your practice, since a journal acts as a reminder. Meditating with others also reinforces your practice. And if you regularly check in with a group or a spiritual partner about how it is going, this will help to keep you on track.

These aids are useful, and you will discover others. Even so, you still must face your resistance to the discipline of meditation.

I've learned a lot about this in recent years. My own resistance to meditation comes and goes, and at first it bewildered me. Usually it takes the form of thinking I have to finish certain tasks before I can meditate. When my regular meditation time comes around, I decide I haven't accomplished enough and can't possibly stop. So I put it off, telling myself I'll meditate later. I deprive myself of the one activity that would restore and rejuvenate me. Why?

Such resistances have no logical base. I easily could carve out fifteen or twenty minutes from my day. Almost everybody can. But I get locked into thinking I have to accomplish yet one more task. My ego attachment to performance is still so strong that it overrides my desire to meditate.

In my wiser moments I understand that my resistance is very much connected to the self-refinement I am doing. My core issue of pride gets played out in this drama involving meditation. I'm so invested in doing something "important" that I forget who I really am and what I really care about. Over time I've become familiar with this resistance. Now I see it more clearly when it surfaces. I don't always change my behavior, but when I do, I rejoice.

You will have your own way of resisting meditating.

Notice it without judgment when it arises. It will be like an overbearing relative—not necessarily the most welcome guest. But after you recognize that it has appeared once again, you can make the decision to go ahead and meditate anyway.

Surviving Meditation Difficulties

All of us have periods when our practices are not going as well as we wish. This is to be expected.

Meditation itself can seem hard to do. Even though we try to follow the instructions we've received, our minds veer off course, jumping from subject to subject with lightning speed. When we bring them back to the task at hand, they rebel. Or we become obsessed with one subject, and can't seem to return to meditation. Or we simply fall asleep.

As a first step, notice what is happening. Become aware of your frenetic mind, your obsessive thinking, or your sleepiness. Then return your attention to the meditation. On hard days you'll have to do this many, many times.

A shift in breathing sometimes helps. If you're having trouble concentrating on the meditation, you can try slowing the pace of your breath for a few minutes. Inhale through your nostrils and exhale through your open mouth. This might be enough to quiet your too active mind so that you can return to the meditation. If you are sleepy, take several short, sharp in-breaths through your nostrils and then exhale. After doing this four or five times, you can then return to the meditation.

Changing the breath does not always help, however. Your difficulty might be coming from the meditation itself. You can try putting aside the one you usually do and selecting another. A shift in focus or a different approach sometimes moves you beyond your current inability to concentrate. But the same difficulty can return once the novelty of the new meditation wears off. If so, recognize that your issue is larger than the meditation itself.

We need to acknowledge the discouragement that can arise when our meditation practices are not going well. At these times we often conclude that something is wrong with us. We compare ourselves to an imaginary "good" meditator, and decide that we are failing.

Keep in mind: There is no such thing as a "good" or "bad" meditator. There are just meditators.

If you are taking the time to meditate, you are a meditator. What happens during a session is of significance to you, but it doesn't factor into your success or failure as a meditator. The person who has a "high" spiritual experience is no better than the one who struggles day after day with distractions.

Discouragement about your performance can make you doubt meditation itself. "I'm no good at meditation" is a close cousin to "meditation is not a useful practice." Be cautious that you don't slide into this judgment. It's important to keep in mind that your personal difficulties are part of the growing experience, and they are no reason to doubt the value of the practice.

For those who become discouraged, the antidote is accepting that the practice is hard at times for everybody, and then going ahead with it anyway. It's essential to trust that you'll get something out of it in the long run.

We cannot conclude this section on meditation difficulties without mentioning another challenge: What should you do when you don't like what you experience while you are meditating?

We sit in the presence of ourselves when we meditate. If our thoughts make us uneasy, this can be uncomfortable. Ordinarily we go through our lives filtering out our deepest impulses, desires, fears, and judgments, but in meditation these things sometimes surface. As I've said, many of us automatically "shut off" if we are flooded by this material. But even a touch of it can be unsettling.

We come upon our inner secrets by surprise in meditation. But this is not the full extent of the challenge. We are also faced with the everyday negative thoughts that exist within us and that are usually ignored. Sometimes when we meditate, we discover we are in the presence of a very unpleasant person, someone who is irritable, or self-righteous, or defensive. As one of my students says about these revelations, "Yuck!"

At one time I obsessed a lot during meditation about my anger toward my sister. She and I were locked into a disagreement about how to care for my seriously ill mother, and I was convinced that I was right. As I meditated I kept repeating my side of the argument to myself. After a while I realized I didn't much care for the self who held such anger. My pettiness and unforgiving spirit were all too obvious to me.

When you don't like what emerges during meditation, you have a few choices. I've found it helpful to simply notice and name what I am thinking. "Here I am again, obsessed with anger," is a good beginning.

If you can develop a wry observer self that comments on your human frailty in a forgiving way, you will be able to meditate without feeling constantly overwhelmed by negative content. "Oy, I'm having such a hard time handling this anger today." Over time you will begin to realize that you, the person, are not the same as you, the holder of thoughts. You will understand that thoughts come and go, but that they are not you. This will help you become more accepting and less judgmental of yourself.

But can we so readily leave behind concern about the content of our thoughts? I don't think so. Meditation is like a litmus test: It reveals the state of our beings. If I notice during meditation that I am filled with anger, this is a warning sign that I need to do something about it. I can look at this anger more carefully and reconsider, say, how I'm acting toward my sister. Then I can find a way to approach her that is more aligned with my values.

But this must be done *after* I've finished meditating. While I'm sitting, my task is to stay with the meditation as much as I can. I do this by bringing my mind away from my anger and directing it to the meditation. Otherwise, my practice becomes jumbled with self-analysis and problem solving.

If you've tried to work with your negative thoughts in this way and you still feel uncomfortable with them, I suggest that you do only focused meditations. They are more structured and provide a stronger focal point for your mind. The *chesed* and *neshamah* meditations are especially good because they will help you become more self-accepting.

In the end it is important to develop an accepting attitude toward these meditation difficulties. We fall into the trap of becoming anxious because we fear we will be deterred from the much desired transformation. But instead, these difficulties are part of the process of transformation, and we grow from them.

Letting Go of Pride

Every meditator struggles with pride. As with doubt, it can cause our practices to falter.

Pride can emerge while we are meditating. We're engrossed in the task, but then we suddenly become conscious of our performance. Our attention switches to how well we're doing, and we compliment ourselves on our success. Immediately we've lost the meditation.

Whenever we become prideful, our ego takes over. The

"I" grows bigger as we declare our success and compare ourselves favorably to other meditators.

Pride is seductive because it makes us feel good. For this same reason, it is hard to catch: We go along without noticing that we have fallen into this state. But soon our practice suffers. When we focus on our accomplishments, we can't enter the silence within. Our minds refuse to let go enough for us to connect with God. We then feel depleted and frustrated. The pleasure of self-importance isn't enough to sustain us.

The best way to diminish pride, I've found, is to become familiar with it. I now recognize the self-promoting voice that takes over my thoughts, telling me how well I am doing as a meditator. "Here it is again," I say. And then I return to the meditation. In some sessions I have to do this repeatedly because I get so caught up in my performance.

Humility requires us to put aside the congratulatory self that intrudes during meditation, and accept that the practice is beyond categories of success or failure. Humility also extends to how we think about ourselves once the meditation session is over. If we rate ourselves as better meditators than others, or think that we are more spiritually evolved than they are, then we are once again being prideful.

One form of meditation is no better than another. Don't fall into the trap of thinking that certain meditative practices are more evolved than others. All forms of meditation can open us to deeper realities, and we need to respect the multitude of pathways. Therefore we shouldn't gloat if we do an *ayin* meditation and move into emptiness while the person next to us does a focused meditation and becomes filled with the presence of God.

In describing pride I do not mean that you should stop feeling good about your meditation practice. It's important to appreciate the work and its results. But there is a difference between loving your practice and getting caught up in your performance as a meditator. The first helps to sustain you, and the second diminishes you and the others around you.

Expanding and Changing Your Practice

Those of you who have used this book to learn to meditate have followed a certain discipline. First you practiced the *hineini* meditation for ten minutes each day. Once this practice became stabilized, you then explored the other core meditations. Some of them probably appealed to you, and others didn't. By now you've settled down with a few favorites.

Through the years I have noticed a wide variety of responses to these meditations. I've tried to understand why certain people are drawn to one and not another. Their reactions seem to come from temperament, life circumstance, and spiritual nature, but I've given up theorizing. In the end these differences are just one more example of the uniqueness of all life.

All of us have our own path. Jewish meditation is not the same for me as it is for you. We learn from others, certainly, but we have to find our own way. The challenge before you is to shape and mold your practice so that it helps you enter the silence within.

As a guideline I've found that it is important to pay attention to how your practice is going. Take the time to acknowledge what you are learning from meditation. Are you getting what you want from it? Is it taking you where you want to go?

It's easy to follow a routine without noticing the subtleties. Those of you who write in journals have a ready-made place to reflect on your experience: You can sift through your thoughts and feelings, and consider their value. But the rest of us have to remember to pay attention to how our practices are going.

This is harder than it sounds. After a certain amount of experimentation in the beginning, most meditators settle into a practice that feels right to them. They become attached to it. You probably have reached this level already: You meditate at a certain time, practicing one or more meditations that you like. This stability is reassuring, and it can last for weeks, months, or even years, with profound results.

But eventually the familiar practice won't quite suit you. You're changing, even if you don't recognize it. Perhaps you'll feel restless, or something will seem to be missing when you meditate. You'll wonder if the problem is within yourself. Perhaps you'll try even harder to make it like it used to be.

Most of us don't want to accept change. We'd rather hold on tightly when faced with it. But at these times your practice needs to be fine-tuned. If you don't do it, you're likely to drop it without good cause, or decide that meditation no longer is useful for you.

Consider trying a new meditation. You can use the ones in this book. In fact, you might discover that one you originally rejected is just right for you now. Or you might ask other people how they meditate and get ideas from them. Or go to workshops or classes on Jewish meditation and learn new meditations. Once you've cultivated a meditation practice, you can choose any meditation you like. Be open to new possibilities.

However, a caveat exists: Take care that you don't fall into the habit of jumping around from meditation to meditation. The goal is to find one, or a few, that work for you—then stay with them. If you change your meditation too often, you will become off-balanced and confused.

You can experiment with meditating at a different time of day. When I switched from morning to late-afternoon meditation, my practice took on a wholly new dimension. In the morning my energy is strong, but later in the day I become more reflective and my mind seems to wander less.

Try meditating in another place. Changing rooms or chairs can be helpful. Sometimes I meditate outside, surrounded and embraced by the natural world. I find that my practice thrives when I do this on occasion.

Another change you can make is to meditate more often. Most of us don't have time for a long meditation session twice a day, but you can take short meditation "time-outs" throughout the day. I know many people who sit in the morning for half an hour, then return to that same meditation for a few minutes in the afternoon and the evening. Imagine starting the day with the *hineini* meditation, then reentering the *hineini* state every so often. This is not hard to do once you've learned how to do it. Those little time-outs can infuse your life with meditative energy. I've taken them in my car in parking lots, in doctors' offices, and in front of my computer.

As you learn more about Judaism you will discover that you can combine other aspects of Jewish spiritual practice with your meditation practice. We'll discuss this in the next chapter, but one example is consciously saying several blessings a day. Your meditation practice will grow as you immerse yourself more fully in a spiritual life.

By now you have gotten the point that it is both legitimate and desirable to fine-tune your meditation practice. I emphasize this because many people assume that Jewish meditation is like those other meditative traditions that require the meditator to stay with one meditation the whole time.

Of course, it is best to be cautious about changing your practice. If it's working, don't alter it. If it isn't, see what you can do to make it better.

There will be periods when you have difficulty concentrating, as we've discussed above. Then, all the fine-tuning in the world won't help that much. When this happens, you need to continue with your regular practice, bringing your mind back to the meditation again and again. Eventually you will get beyond your difficulties.

Balancing Your Practice with the Rest of Your Life

People come to Jewish meditation already involved in relationships, work, and communities. They hold values and they have commitments. When they begin meditating they often are surprised by the power of the practice. For some, it not only transforms their consciousness but affects the very fabric of their lives.

The challenge, then, is to negotiate this change in a sensitive and responsible way.

Many meditators find that they are less satisfied with their previous associations and commitments. A long-term student of mine says it succinctly: "I'm not who I used to be." A woman in her fifties, she has been proud of her secular identity all her adult life. But now she is deeply immersed in Jewish meditation, and she studies Judaism and spends time with other meditators. Suddenly she isn't secular anymore. This change bewilders her. It involves both loss and gain: "My old friends no longer interest me in the same way, and I feel guilty. I'm getting so much from meditation, but they fail to understand. They wonder what happened to the woman they knew." I do not underestimate her feeling of dislocation. I've heard it before from others who enthusiastically take up the meditative path.

I advise beginning meditators to go slowly. Although their involvement in meditation is a pleasure to witness, I know that it can lead to premature rejection of a previous life. It's not a good idea to throw away anything that has had meaning in the past. Certain habits, values, and life pursuits will shift over time. But it's best to let this change happen on its own accord rather than to do it arbitrarily with the first burst of enthusiasm.

When we take on a meditation practice, those closest to us can feel threatened. This is understandable, because a new element is being introduced into the relationship. We're involved in a spiritual pursuit that can be life-changing, and our partners, children, or friends sense its importance. They might fear that they'll lose us. If they don't meditate themselves, they possibly don't understand or approve of what we're doing.

The beginning meditator needs to find a way to reassure important others that they will not be abandoned because of the practice. The first step is to be clear within yourself about your commitment to the relationship. Assuming that it is strong, you then need to monitor yourself to make sure you don't exude judgment or snobbery, or cause others to feel inadequate because they do not meditate. If you use meditation as a tool against them, they will resent your involvement.

Your task is to be sensitive to those you love. These relationships must be nourished and appreciated, and you should be careful that your practice does not become an issue. On occasion, however, troubled relationships come apart and meditation is blamed as the "last straw." If this happens, it is very sad. You need to look at your own behavior and learn from it. If you find yourself thinking that the problem came about because of your spiritual growth—and your "superiority"—as a meditator, you are being irresponsible. You also are missing an opportunity to do some important work within yourself.

Integrating meditation into our lives becomes complicated at times. It obviously affects close relationships more than others. Still, we find that most people appear different to us than before we began to meditate. We are becoming more aware, and thereby we more easily see both the beauty and the limitations of those around us. The question is how to keep our hearts open to others when they are not going down the same path that we are.

Hopefully, Jewish meditation will help you become a more loving person over time. As you begin to work through your negative personality traits and diminish their effects, you will be less defensive. Instead of getting caught up in power struggles with others, you'll stay uninvolved. This is not to say that you will care less for those around you: You'll care even more because you will have a greater capacity to love.

People who are insecure need others to follow the same path that they are on. But as you meditate, you will become more fully the person you can be. You won't demand that others mirror you or join you every step along the way. As you grow through meditation, you'll be able to see other people as separate beings, and respect their paths in life. Finally, you will love them more fully because you will allow them to be themselves, not a reflection of you.

Another aspect of balancing meditation with the rest of your life has to do with how you spend your time. Sometimes beginning meditators decide that they should refrain from those things that used to bring them pleasure. B-movie videos, or sports events, or computer games, or shopping sprees get tossed out in an attempt to act in a more meditative way. If this change comes about because you really are no longer interested in these things, that's fine. But if you are trying to live up to an internalized image of "spiritual person" or "dedicated meditator," then it's not a good idea.

No matter how much we meditate, we still are a part of this world. Judaism strongly stresses that we cannot transcend our humanness in our lifetimes, and we shouldn't even try. Activities that bring us pleasure are good—as long as we act in a responsible way.

Through meditation you will find that your ability to truly enjoy yourself will increase. You will be more alive. Your laughter will deepen and your smile will broaden. The image of the stern-faced contemplative just doesn't hold. The quietness of meditation gives birth to joyful activity, not solemnity.

Living Your Practice

Jewish meditation embodies the belief that all life is holy. We are connected to each other and to all beings, and our task is to help heal the brokenness that exists in this world.

One of the challenges of Jewish meditation is to bring this understanding into the rest of your life. It's easy to go about your regular routine in the same old way after you meditate. When you do this, however, meditation becomes a garment that you slip on for a limited time, then put away after use. The question is how to make your life more congruent with your meditation practice.

I have suggested that it's a mistake to cut yourself off precipitously from those people and activities that meant something to you before you began to meditate. The tendency of beginners is to get caught up in the image of being a meditator, and go overboard with change.

I do not mean, however, that you should continue your life exactly as you lived it before. You can trust that meditation will help you become more aware and sensitive to others over time. Without your active direction, you'll experience subtle shifts. Still, it is essential that you pay conscious attention to what you are doing right now in your life.

Gaps exist between what we believe and how we live. Often they are unintentional: We simply haven't thought through the details carefully enough. For instance, it took me a long time to realize that my belief in treating everyone with dignity should extend to the salespeople who telephone me at home during dinner. When they called, I scolded them or slammed down the phone. After several especially nasty calls, I was uncomfortable with my behavior; it didn't jibe with the quality of respectful appreciation that I was cultivating during meditation. I realized that I needed to act differently—or acknowledge that I was a hypocrite. I then had to think about how I would handle the situation in the future. My choices were to turn off the phone or decide what to say ahead of time so that my annoyance at being disturbed wouldn't make me act disrespectfully.

Beginning meditators sometimes fear that they'll suffer if they don't express every anger. This concern comes from the popular idea in our culture that repressed emotions cause mental and physical distress. But those of us who follow the Jewish meditation spiritual path know that another option exists. Our model is to become aware of what we feel and to name it silently to ourselves. *Then* we decide what we are going to do with it. Sometimes the feeling is best shared, and sometimes it's not.

We have far more choice over our behavior than we ordinarily assume. As a result of the awareness that comes through meditation, we can decide to act in accordance with our beliefs. I've found that meditation has helped me become aware of my feelings and express them more clearly. Rather than overwhelming others with my irritation or slinking around resentfully, I more often use anger in a constructive way.

Another aspect of living our practices is service to others. Earlier I described the Jewish concept of *tikkun olam,* healing the world. This is an underlying value of Jewish meditation.

If we wait to be inspired to do service, we might never get around to it. Therefore we need to look carefully at what we do with our time and our resources. Should we make a greater effort to volunteer for worthy projects? Should we spend our money in different ways? How can we use our particular talents to bring about healing? These are some of the questions we ask ourselves.

As our hearts open through meditation, we care more about the pain in the world and feel called upon to help others.

But we have to be careful that we don't burn out. Meditation helps us with this by keeping us balanced and saving us from becoming overextended. It restores us so that we are replenished at the same time that we are giving. Through meditation we find the strength to continue making our contribution to the world.

Continuing Self-refinement

Self-refinement, as I've said, goes on for a lifetime. It's never completed. However, the process itself is transformative, and we change along the way. Our souls become more translucent and radiant as we become less bound by our destructive qualities.

The idea of self-refinement usually resonates with students, and they understand its importance. But the sheer weight of our shortcomings can be overwhelming. Our greed, envy, excessive anger, stubbornness, irresponsibility, and so forth, seem too hard to change. The challenge is to continue the work, even when we become discouraged.

Meditation is a good place to begin this work. We can't help but bump into our negative tendencies in our practices. They show up in the content of our resistances to meditation and in the content of our thoughts while we're sitting. After a while we become very familiar with them.

One of my students has a habit of self-pity: He resists meditation by telling himself that it's too hard and he can't possibly do it. Then, when he meditates, he pores over all the hurtful things that have happened recently, examining every detail, feeling sorry for himself. He avoids awareness of this habit of self-pity in his everyday life, but he can't escape it during meditation.

Another student is attached to envy. She compares herself to other meditators, thinking that they must have an easier time than she does, or that they are doing it better. Her mind keeps returning to all those things that she lacks, even though she is privileged and successful in her work and in her life.

Meditation helps us learn more about ourselves. We come to see the negative states of mind that emerge day after day. Certainly all of us are angry, or fearful, or prideful at certain times. Our life events call forth these responses. But if one of these becomes the grand theme of your meditative experience and you keep noticing it, you know it is part of refining yourself.

We must take care that we don't become judgmental about our negative qualities. We all have them, and yours are no better or worse than anyone else's. Even though you might not like them, they are at the core of your work.

During meditation we learn to recognize and accept their existence without becoming entangled in them. We notice them, then return to the task of meditation. A danger exists if we don't do this: We can get stuck in our fascination with our own shortcomings and exaggerate them so that they become enormously important in our minds. This increases their hold over us.

When you are *not* meditating, you can examine a troublesome trait more carefully: Where did it come from? How does it play itself out in your life? Under what circumstances does it arise? How does it affect others around you?

The point is to gather information about this shortcoming rather than try to erase it—which is impossible. You simply are becoming more familiar with it. This is an important first step in accepting responsibility for your own change.

Once you are familiar with a negative trait, you can work on it. When you notice it popping up in your daily life or within yourself, you can choose to act differently. The self-pitying person doesn't always need to complain about hardships. The angry person has alternatives to obsessing about retribution. Over time this trait will diminish, although it never will entirely go away. We remain imperfect, despite our desire to come to completion.

Students often ask about the relationship of self-refinement to psychotherapy. In our culture many of us have been in therapy, or at least we consider it as an option in difficult times.

Therapy can be helpful in answering some of your questions about a troublesome trait. Through self-examination you can begin to see its genesis and the difficulty it creates for you and those around you. A therapist's presence can support you as you more honestly look at yourself. Those of you who experienced severe childhood trauma will especially benefit from therapy as an adjunct to self-refinement, because it can help you establish a base of trust and move away from the despair of childhood wounds.

My only concern about psychotherapy is that it sometimes tends to emphasize the past rather than root itself in the present and the future. We can spend years sifting through our previous relationships and traumas while ignoring who we are today and where we are going.

Self-refinement is directed toward the future. The point is for us to become more fully the people we can be so that we contribute increasingly to *tikkun olam.* If we feel better or are happier as a result of this work, that's a blessing. But it's not the aim.

Many psychotherapists understand the spiritual journey

and will be able to work with you. You should make sure you choose one of these therapists if you decide to go into therapy.

Many of you won't consult a therapist, however. Self-refinement doesn't require professional help. But you'll find it useful to discuss your process with others at opportune times. Most meditation teachers have had experience with this work, and spiritual counselors, now found in many locations, can guide you in the process. Your rabbi or other spiritual leader might or might not understand your concerns, depending on his or her training and sensitivity to spiritual issues.

If you have a meditation partner, bring up the subject. Or open it up in your meditation group. You also might find it helpful to speak about it with those close to you, even if they are not meditators. For example, I have discussed my overdeveloped pride with my grown children. The more I learn about it, the more insight I can share, and my children appreciate the opportunity to offer their wisdom and support. My honesty enables them to look at how the issue has affected them too.

Conversations about self-refinement are not meant to be heavy and psychological. Rather, they have a descriptive quality: I am aware that I get caught up in my pride, and it manifests itself in many ways. With the help of others I try to see it more clearly so that it has less of a hold over my actions and my inner experience.

Self-refinement is an important part of Jewish meditation. It's the way we become sturdier vessels for the light of God. The more we do it, the more we are able to be present in each moment. Our meditation deepens because we are less bound by our negative states of mind.

10

Meditation and Jewish Spiritual Practice

In past centuries Jewish meditators embraced a lifestyle that revolved entirely around traditional Jewish observance, including the spiritual practices of Shabbat, *mitzvot,* Torah study, and prayer. It would have been unthinkable to meditate without paying attention to these other aspects of Jewish practice.

Today, many meditators are not traditionally observant. The reasons are varied: They don't like Orthodoxy's treatment of women, or they don't know enough about traditional Judaism to practice it, or they are intimidated by all its requirements, or they are more comfortable in liberal or progressive settings. Fortunately, we live in a time and a place where we can choose how we want to be Jewish. Nobody is forcing us to behave in a more rigorously observant way.

Still, a question exists: How can beginners integrate meditation into the rest of Judaism without the knowledge that comes from years of study, and without the practice guidelines that exist in Orthodoxy? They don't know where to start.

But their uncertainty doesn't last for long. Jewish

meditation is so infused with Jewish content that most beginning meditators become interested in learning more about it. One discovery leads to another. As they pick up knowledge they expand their practice to include other aspects of Jewish observance. They might decide to light candles in a meditative way on Friday night, or to say a blessing before eating. Meditation often remains their primary spiritual path, but once they discover other possibilities, they add them to their practices.

And why not? Judaism is rich with ways to make our lives more spiritually meaningful. We can decide which ones we want to explore.

We need to learn as much as we can about Judaism and its ways of spiritual connection so that we can incorporate them into our lives. As meditators this will strengthen our practices. I encourage you to take classes in Jewish observance, to read about it, and to talk with others who have had more experience with Judaism. Check out the list of books at the end of this book; they will help you increase your knowledge about Judaism.

Often students go through a period of Jewish immersion when they absorb as much as they can. They might not choose to observe certain traditional practices, such as *kashrut* (the dietary laws of Judaism), but they find other practices that fit in with their beliefs and their lifestyles. Or they modify traditional practices to add spiritual meaning to their lives. For example, they might change their eating habits so that they more clearly reflect their concern about the environment and the treatment of animals.

Once you begin to learn more about Judaism, you can consider how to combine Jewish practice with meditation. In this chapter I describe several important Jewish practices, and suggest ways to do this.

The following discussion is just a beginning. Shelves of books have been written about each of these spiritual practices, so at best, I can only introduce them to you. Through your study you will come to understand that Judaism is a beautiful religion, offering many possibilities for finding spiritual meaning.

Your task is to bring meditative awareness into the exploration of Shabbat, or prayer, or *mitzvot,* or any of the other practices. Experience them, then decide how to include them in your life.

The Practice of Shabbat

We begin with Shabbat, the most central spiritual practice of Judaism. Shabbat is a day of rest, the holiest day of the week. It starts on Friday at sundown and ends on Saturday night, when three stars become visible in the sky.

People who observe Shabbat know its incredible beauty. When I first learned about it, I couldn't believe it was true. A commandment to rest and restore ourselves? Surely this was a contradiction. It's like saying we are commanded to eat the most delicious food, or forced to watch the most gorgeous sunset.

Shabbat reminded me of when my mother decided to contain our childhood consumption of sweets by declaring one day a week as "candy day." Six days, no candy, and then on the seventh, we could eat as much as we wanted. I could hardly wait for this day to arrive. And then: the smoothness on my tongue and the feeling of euphoria.

In this way I learned to respect the buildup of desire, and then its fulfillment. Six days of ordinary consciousness moving toward Shabbat—and then Shabbat. They complement each other and form a perfect whole.

Shabbat gives us twenty-four hours away from the rush of our everyday lives. It is an island in time, as Abraham Joshua Heschel wrote. A day on which we are not meant to worry, or plan, or argue. Just to be present in the moment. Surely this is the greatest meditation of all.

This detachment from our everyday lives is not always entirely possible, but we strive for it. On Shabbat we are encouraged to enjoy ourselves with food, wine, friends, family, lovemaking, meditation, prayer, and study. The day is a retreat from the world. The traditional rules of Shabbat might seem strict—they legislate against doing anything that can be construed as work—but they keep us in this altered state. Could there be greater pleasure?

Yet many of us resist Shabbat. We don't want to be taken out of our everyday lives. We don't want to postpone completing another task, or buying another item, or being entertained. Friday night and Saturday are prime weekend hours, and we are used to filling them with activities, even though our bodies and spirits yearn for rest.

Orthodox Jews understand the power of Shabbat because they observe it fully. By not driving, not cooking, not cleaning, not writing, and by observing all the other "nots," they move into Shabbat consciousness.

But those of us who haven't experienced Shabbat hardly know what it is like—unless we meditate. Meditators can sense its meaning even if we haven't experienced it because there is a connection between Shabbat and meditation. Both practices take us out of the world and beyond ordinary consciousness. We don't need to be convinced of the value of this experience.

I encourage you to embrace Shabbat fully. However, if this seems too extreme, start with Friday evening alone.

It's best to decide what you are going to do before Shabbat begins, rather than after it starts. That way you don't have to figure it out moment by moment. If you don't wish to talk on the phone during Shabbat, turn it off before sundown on Friday. If you want to take a hike with a friend on Saturday afternoon, make arrangements ahead of time.

Some of you will follow the complete Orthodox practice on Shabbat. Others will not. Once you grasp the concept, you can set it up as you wish. One of my friends always removes her watch as the sun goes down on Friday night, and she stays home alone, meditating. On Saturday she visits friends, or runs errands, or goes to the movies. Although she's not strictly observing Shabbat, she is reminded of it every time she notices her missing watch, and she continues to feel the sweetness of being slightly outside of time. Another friend likes to have a big Shabbat dinner with his family, then collapse into bed. On Saturday morning he goes to services, and in the afternoon, on sunny days, he takes a few hours for a meditative retreat, climbing the hill behind his house and sitting in the craggy nook of a large oak tree.

You will find your own rhythms. As Shabbat approaches, I love to prepare for it by cooking and by making the house beautiful. My husband shares these tasks, so it's a time of growing closeness between us. Finally, we light the candles, and I feel myself begin to let go of the week and settle into the holy space of Shabbat. The hours after that are filled with joy, pleasure, and contentment.

I especially love to meditate on Shabbat, since I'm already in a state of openness. My meditation on Saturday morning usually is organized around words from the prayers: I like to do the *modah ani* and *neshamah* meditations, and I include others I've drawn from the liturgy. If I don't go to services, this is my way of combining prayer and meditation.

The aim of all this is to experience Shabbat in a meditative state. Each of us must determine how to do it. One of my students meditates on the Shabbat candles, lighting them slowly, then focusing her attention on them as they burn. Another loves to drum and chant late into the night with her partner. A beloved colleague meditates by reflecting over his unresolved issues, then letting them dissolve. Finally, he moves into utter silence.

Candles. Light. Song. Prayer. Silence. Regeneration. It's all there for you to discover. Do it, if you can, with others. It becomes even more powerful that way. But if you are alone, your Shabbat can also be filled with joy and pleasure. You too will find that meditation on Shabbat is the greatest gift.

The Observance of Holidays

Judaism is a calendar religion, organized around the phases of the moon and the seasons of the year. On the first day of each new moon we celebrate Rosh Hodesh. This is a minor holiday, marked in synagogues by the announcement of the new month and special prayers. Women, especially, like to gather at this time to study and celebrate because of the moon's association with the monthly menstrual cycle.

I vividly remember when I first heard about the significance of the moon in Judaism. I was attending a class on Jewish practice, and the teacher asked what phase the moon was in that night. None of us could answer. He then said that the moon cycle is one of the most powerful rhythms in Judaism, and we should pay attention to it. Just as Shabbat comes once a week, Rosh Hodesh arrives every month.

Since then I have kept track of the moon. I know that my subtle energies are connected to its waxing and waning. I like to observe Rosh Hodesh by meditating. It is a time of beginnings: That which is hidden is ready to emerge, but is not yet present. On this night I feel vulnerable and even a little afraid. Yet I know that the darkness of the sky will not last, and the moon's light soon will be revealed. I also feel excited because of the possibilities I sense in the month ahead.

You too can try to bring these images into your meditation. Take some time to yourself, and experience that moment when the moon is birthed anew and darkness gives way to light.

Judaism is blessed with many holidays. Just as the lunar cycles are observed in Judaism, so too are the seasons. In the spring we celebrate Pesach (Passover). In the summer, Shavuot. In the fall, Sukkot. These holidays follow the cycle of nature by marking the early growth of spring crops, the summer abundance, and the final harvest.

The seasonal holidays are far more complex than calendar markers, however. As anyone who has participated in a seder knows, Pesach is the story of freedom from bondage and triumph over oppression. The lessons are deep. And if we look at the mystical meanings of the holiday—the passage through the Red Sea as our own rebirth, or the Pharaoh as our own core negative tendencies, for example—we have enough material to contemplate for several seasons.

Each holiday has layers and layers of meaning. Each year I encounter Pesach with fresh eyes and it gives me new insight.

Other holidays in the Jewish calendar include Rosh Hashanah, Yom Kippur, Simchat Torah, Hanukkah, Tu Bishevat, Purim, and Tisha b'Av. For some of you these are unfamiliar names, but once you begin to explore the days of observance, they will come alive with meaning.

You can choose which holidays you want to integrate into your life. Immerse yourself in them and learn about them. You'll find knowledge and wisdom in the books on holidays in the Jewish meditation resource guide at the end of the book.

Holidays are meant to be experienced with others. So find people who will join you, or look for a congregation or community that suits you. Bring your imagination and creativity to Jewish holidays. We share the same Pesach, but everyone perceives it differently. When we discuss our interpretations at the seder table, we learn from each other.

Let your meditations flow from the images in the holidays. Before Pesach take the time to prepare for the experience by contemplating the journey ahead. And during the holiday make sure that you set aside time to focus on the vision of rebirth. Or on the joy of Miriam's dance after crossing the Red Sea. Or on the image of God being present as you move from slavery to freedom.

When you begin to observe the holidays, your life will be greatly enriched. The secular calendar will seem pale in comparison. Celebrating with others will draw you more into community. And meditating alone will make the experience even stronger.

The Study of Torah

We usually think of study as an intellectual pursuit or a left-brain activity that involves our reasoning faculties. Torah study can be a spiritual experience, however. I remember when I first discovered this. I was living in a traditional Orthodox household, and we used to read the weekly portion of the Torah together in English. We'd linger over the parts that engaged our imaginations, and as the images and ideas emerged, I became excited, even if I didn't agree with the text. My mind expanded and moved in creative directions, and I experienced new thoughts and perceptions. Surprisingly, this felt spiritual to me.

The Torah can be approached in various ways. On the *peshat* (translated as "literal") level we simply follow the narrative. This is a good exercise for those who are unacquainted with the contents of the Torah. On the *remez* ("hint") level we look for veiled allusions to deeper meaning. For instance, we notice words that are repeated, or left out, or strangely expressed. On the *drash* ("interpretive") level we elaborate and associate with the text in order to understand it. Through the centuries poetic interpretations of Torah called *midrash* have been written, for example. And finally, on the *sod* ("mystery") level we read the text to glimpse and experience the presence of the Divine in the world.

No one way of studying Torah is best. These days I like to scan the whole weekly portion so that I recall what is in it, and then I concentrate on a few words or verses that intrigue me. I free-associate with them, opening up their meaning, stretching them as far as I can. Often I join with others to do this because I am stimulated by their ideas. Or I read interpretations of this text. Usually I come away from this study in a heightened state, refreshed and invigorated. The Divine is very present in these moments.

Through the exercise of the mind in Torah study, we jump off into the unknown. There are no "right" interpretations or "best" answers in this practice. We don't have to like or accept the text. The point is to be entirely present with the words and make ourselves available to them.

Torah study can have a meditative quality. Like the focused meditations we do, it requires us to keep our minds on the subject. When our thoughts wander, we draw them back to the words in Torah.

Some people like to meditate before studying Torah. They say that this connects them to the Divine and helps them experience the words of Torah in a more immediate way. Others meditate afterwards because they are in an open state from the study of Torah.

I often draw material for meditations from the Torah. For example, the image of the *mishkan* (portable sanctuary) can be used as a focus. The book of Exodus describes this intricate and beautiful dwelling place of God, built by the Hebrew people in the desert after experiencing the revelation at Mount Sinai. I like to teach that we all have a *mishkan* within, a holy place that is ours to nourish and maintain. During meditation we can direct our breath to it, or envision it, or feel its presence and draw strength from it. Or we simply can say *hineini*.

THE PRACTICE OF PRAYER

Prayer is our way of communicating with God. We raise our voices, or chant softly, or pray silently to convey what is in our hearts.

Meditation is the way we enter the silence within. Although God is not directly addressed in this practice, we experience profound moments of union with the Holy and the dissolution of the individual self, just as we do in prayer.

The two practices are very close. At times they seem to merge. Prayer can be experienced as meditative, and meditation can be experienced as prayerful.

I discovered the meditative quality of prayer when I first attended three-hour Shabbat services at an Orthodox *shul.* The Hebrew words of the prayers, chanted by the congregants, seemed like a mantra to me. I didn't understand what they meant at that time, but it didn't matter. As I hummed along, I became so filled with the sound that I dropped into a deep meditative state. Since then I've learned that many other people have this experience.

Prayer and meditation can be combined in many ways. For example, some people meditate before they pray. One of my teachers used to say that the best way for him to enter prayer was to meditate for an hour beforehand. Then, he *really* was ready to begin. Like most of us, he seldom had the time to do this, but even ten minutes of meditation can make prayer more meaningful.

Another way of combining meditation and prayer is found in some Sephardi Orthodox synagogues where congregants take a meditative break during the prayer services if they find they are not paying attention. Typically they go to a *shivitti,* an ornamental design of Hebrew words and Biblical phrases hanging on the wall, and gaze at the words until one or more leap out at them. Then they focus on these words in meditation until their distraction ceases and they are ready to return to prayer.

We too can integrate meditation into prayer. If I find I am mechanically repeating the liturgy, I like to choose a word or phrase from one of the prayers and meditate with it. To make the meditation even more powerful, I wrap my *tallit* (prayer shawl) over my head so that I am in a private space. For months I focused this way on the God-word "Redeemer," and layers of its meaning were revealed to me.

Some people meditate immediately after prayer as a way to prolong the energy that comes from the experience. Rather than returning immediately to their daily lives, they savor these moments: They are in a state of oneness with God, and they want to stay there for a while longer.

Sometimes people spontaneously switch into prayer after meditation because they are so moved by their experience. "Thank you, God!" is a natural ending to a meditation of great strength. Or they speak silently to God during their meditation because they experience the Divine presence so intensely.

You probably are beginning to see how meditation and prayer can go together. I've described only a few ways, but there are many more. Whether you pray alone or with others, you can experiment with combining the two.

Some of you might not want to pray, or you are unfamiliar with the Jewish liturgy. Even so, you might consider opening a *siddur* (Jewish prayer book) or the book of Psalms, and picking out a word or phrase for meditation. Even if you don't feel comfortable with most of the content of the prayers, you will find a word or phrase that works for you. Simply hold it in your mind and focus your attention on it, using the same technique as you do with other focused meditations. When your mind wanders, bring it back to the words.

The Blessings Path

Many of us are familiar with the Hebrew words *Baruch Ata Adonai* (pronounced "ba-rook ah-ta ah-doe-nahy"). These words mean "Blessed are You, God." They are traditionally followed by other words, such as in the blessing over wine: *Baruch Ata Adonai, Eloheinu Melekh ha-olam, borei pre hagafen,* which means "Blessed are You, God, Sovereign of the universe, Who births the fruit of the vine."

When we bless the Divine for each thing that we receive, we acknowledge these gifts in our lives. We also name their Source. The wine doesn't originate in the bottle; it ultimately comes from the Source of all Life. The sun's warmth and the change of seasons are beyond human control, and we remind ourselves of this.

The Talmud's instructions to say one hundred blessings a day is for our benefit: God doesn't "need" them, but *we* do. We so often fail to pay attention to what comes to us. Our awareness extends only to the most general or obvious things, such as a prosperous year or the birth of a child.

I once went on a walk with an observant woman who follows the spiritual practice of saying blessings. Our conversation frequently paused as she spied a bed of flowers, or a jagged rock, or the smile of a young woman, and exclaimed, "*Baruch HaShem*"—Blessed is the Name! When she spoke of seeing her cousin in the hospital, and of the struggle she's had with her son's learning disorder, she also said, "*Baruch HaShem.*" At first these interjections seemed strange, but I soon fell into their rhythm. It wasn't as hard as you might think. The result was that I noticed more of what was going on around me, and I felt a deeper appreciation for it. My blessings included those things that were challenging or even painful, as well as those that were more easily seen as gifts.

The blessings path is directed toward blessing the Divine. But it also includes blessing other people. A man I know, a spiritual leader in my community, does this every day: He inserts a blessing in the course of a conversation, in a greeting or parting, or as he passes someone in the street. Almost everyone receives one. His blessings are sensitive and subtle, a welcome relief from the automatic "Have a nice day." He absorbs the presence of the other person and lets his words come from a place of intuitive wisdom. Usually he vocalizes the deepest yearnings of the other, such as "Bless you, my friend, that the ache in your heart dissolves and you find peace."

Another part of the practice of blessings is to bless people or objects—instead of God—for what they give to us: "I bless you, tree, for teaching me perseverance against the winter storms." "I bless you, my child, for helping me learn patience."

Blessings cultivate awareness. We first have to notice what we receive before we say them. If I am unaware, I don't know what to bless.

I've found that beginning meditators appreciate the blessings path because it increases their awareness. It also makes them feel more connected to everything around them. As a spiritual practice it is easy to do, and it brings them a sense of satisfaction. Those who struggle with negative thoughts during meditation find that they become less preoccupied with all the things that are going wrong or they are lacking.

A good first step is to commit yourself to saying five blessings a day. Use your own words, or find traditional or nontraditional God-language that you like. It's important to say your blessings with *kavvanah*—if you dash them off too quickly, you might as well not bother.

Some students like to pick five blessings and say the same ones each day. These might include meal blessings or selections from the blessings found in the liturgy. Others like to do them spontaneously, responding to the daily flow of events. Once you become grounded in giving blessings in this way, you can expand your practice.

Try saying blessings as you drive from one place to another. Give one to every person you pass and every thing you notice. Or say them silently to yourself during a meeting. Or say one within your heart to a particularly difficult person.

Over time a practice of blessings will enrich your meditative life. If you are in a state of awareness of the gifts you receive, you will be more spiritually attuned as you go about your daily affairs. As a result, your presence increasingly will be a blessing to others.

The Practice of *Mitzvot*

The word *mitzvot* refers to the 613 commandments found in Judaism. Observant Jews are committed to living by these laws as best as they can. The laws encompass most aspects of behavior, including how to treat strangers, how to resolve business quarrels, how to relate to family members, and how to fulfill Jewish ritual obligation. This prescribed way of life requires discipline and diligence, and traditional Jews consider it to be a central Jewish practice.

Those of us who are not Orthodox can embrace the spiritual practice of *mitzvot,* even though we do it in a nontraditional way. This means trying to live our lives in as loving, constructive, and ethical a way as possible. We don't feel compelled to obey all the rules of Jewish law, but we're concerned about how we act toward others. We attempt to improve our behavior so that we contribute more to the world.

This aim sounds good, but we often don't know how best to fulfill it. It's hardest of all when someone angers or frustrates us, or when we are dealing with ambiguities that confuse us. If we're Orthodox, we look for answers in books on Jewish law or we consult our rabbi. Those of us who don't live by Jewish law, however, wonder what guidelines to use. Without such parameters, we often feel adrift.

I suggest, then, that you investigate the tradition's teachings about *mitzvot.* You'll find some interesting ideas there that can help you clarify your own values. For example, one law says that it's forbidden to put a stumbling block in front of a person who can't see. This means that we shouldn't tempt people to do things that might be hurtful to them. The braggart at a party, for example, should not be encouraged to talk about himself, because he'll only end up alienating people by his exaggerated stories. The loving act is to lead him into another topic of conversation, even though he resists it. That way we are not participating in his rejection.

Jewish law offers guidance about seemingly insignificant behavior. Idle gossip, for instance, is shown to be destructive far beyond our usual understanding. In one rabbinic story it is likened to letting loose the feathers from a goose-down pillow: They float in the breeze, away from us, and never can be retrieved.

The practice of *mitzvot* requires us to evaluate our actions. Can we contribute more to those around us? In what ways? We need to think carefully about these questions and make decisions about how we intend to act.

If we embrace a practice of *mitzvot,* we will emphasize performing acts of *chesed,* loving-kindness. We don't wait to be asked. When we are irritable or tired, we still feel the responsibility to do this: The practice is not an on-again, off-again matter, dependent on our mood. We don't expect to be perfect—nobody is. But we stretch toward being the kind of people that we have decided we should be.

There will be times when we need to draw back from this practice. We can't give to others if we are physically or emotionally exhausted. The practice doesn't mean that we let ourselves be used in ways that hurt us. We must guard against our own depletion. An act of kindness done with a resentful expression or a sigh is not a kindness at all. Rather, its mixed message confuses the receiver and it might as well not be offered.

Meditation is an enormous support for those who practice *mitzvot*. It provides inner sustenance and helps us remember why we are doing this work. In times of stress we emerge from meditation with a renewed sense of commitment.

The *chesed* meditation can be especially helpful with this practice because it opens our hearts. Often we want to reach out in compassion, but it is hard to do it with people who frustrate or disappoint us, or whom we don't like. Meditation gives us enough distance from the struggle of personality so that we can act in a more loving way toward everyone.

The Practice of *Tikkun Olam*

Many of us yearn to bridge the gap between our everyday lives and our spiritual practices. We've already suggested one possibility: the practice of *mitzvot. Tikkun olam* is another.

As a people, Jews are known for their commitment to healing and repairing the world. This value is embraced as part of our tradition. But imagine taking on *tikkun olam* as a spiritual practice. If you were to do this, you would direct more of your time, energy, and resources to healing the world. You would commit yourself to greater involvement. This might mean becoming more politically active, or volunteering at a local nonprofit organization, or contributing a larger percentage of your salary to *tzedakah* (charitable contributions), or even changing the nature of your work. *Tikkun olam* calls for an attitude of caring about what is going on around you.

I know many students whose main spiritual practice is *tikkun olam*. They feel a deep spiritual connection with others through this work, and experience the strong presence of the holiness of all life. They embrace history as the movement toward a better world where all beings live in harmony, and they join with all the generations before them who participated in this effort.

Many of these people are not religious, at least in the traditional sense. But their commitment to this practice is profoundly Jewish in that they believe that rightful action is more important than all the words we utter.

For those of you who make *tikkun olam* a spiritual practice, meditation can be extremely helpful. I suggest that you take time to do it regularly. Because of the demands of this work, you must guard against becoming spiritually drained. Meditation can help replenish you.

If you can, find others who are engaged in *tikkun olam* and meditate with them. You'll discover that your conversations about this practice and the issues that arise will give you strength.

Putting It All Together

The spiritual practice of *tikkun olam* is a fitting end to this book. Meditation, after all, is about us refining ourselves and becoming transformed so that we can make a greater contribution to the world. Some of us will commit ourselves to *tikkun olam* as a spiritual practice and make significant changes in the way we live. Others of us won't. But all of us have the responsibility to think carefully about how we act and what we do. Our behavior must be informed by the insights that we receive through meditation.

Jewish meditation can help us become more aware, more focused, and more spiritually attuned, and it can bring us closer to God. But what is the point of meditation if we do not apply this understanding to the way we live?

In the *hineini* meditation we become present by focusing on "Here I am." We move into a passive state so that we are spiritually open. When our minds become active, we quiet them. This passivity is appropriate during meditation, but when meditation is over, it is time to act on what we've experienced. We are ready to make choices. We must do our self-refinement, because we know that meditation alone is not enough to make us better people.

The spiritual path of Jewish meditation can be transformative, but only if we accept the responsibility of doing the work that goes along with it. Transformation is revealed by small shifts of behavior in our daily lives, not by sweeping statements about how much we've changed. It shows up in how we treat our children, how we care for the earth, and how we resolve our quarrels.

This understanding of transformation comes from the Jewish tradition. In Judaism we strive to become more compassionate and just, and to take responsibility for those who are less fortunate than ourselves. Even the smallest actions toward others have consequences, and therefore are significant.

Judaism prescribes a course of action to guide us in this effort to improve our behavior. The spiritual practices described in this chapter are meant to do that. Even if we don't observe them in the traditional way, they supplement and support the work of meditation.

Jewish meditation, then, finds its place along with the other spiritual practices in Judaism. And when we combine them, so that, for instance, prayer or Shabbat or the holidays are done in a meditative way, they each become stronger. And in the end they help us become greater vessels of holiness in this world.

11

A Morning Meditative Prayer Practice

Once you know how to meditate, you can explore putting meditation together with prayer in creative ways. This section introduces you to one example. This practice, which I do daily, is based on the Jewish morning prayer service, *shacharit.*

Some background material: Practicing Jews pray *shacharit* every morning, whether it is a weekday, Shabbat, or holiday. The service is basically the same from day to day—although there is variety in the number of prayers, psalms, and readings included depending on the day, and sometimes there are special sections added to the *Amidah,* the long personal prayer.

The basic structure of the service remains, bringing a person through many different stages, or levels, of awareness and consciousness during its course. This progression is the base for my morning practice. I've built it around the stages that are inherent in every *shacharit* service and made it into a practice that I find meaningful. Not everything in the service is included—it would take way too long—but the essential parts are here.

Sometimes I take forty-five minutes or an hour to do this

practice, but that's the exception. Like most people, I'm busy, so most often I do it in ten to fifteen minutes.

I've found that this practice marks my days with gratitude and intention, and is essential to my feeling of spiritual well-being. If I forget to do it, which happens once in a while, I notice the difference—a certain tightness, a certain lack of connection. I've been practicing it for over ten years now and can't imagine my life without it.

Think of this practice as moving from one reality to another, seven altogether. As you go through each one, the point is to dwell within it for at least a few minutes, focusing your mind and your awareness, holding the intention. As always with meditation, if your mind wanders, let go of your thoughts and bring your mind back to the intention. You will be able to use the meditative skills you've developed to intensify your experience. When you are finished, you'll feel ready to move into your day with awareness and purpose.

I find that the setting for this practice is important. I usually sit or stand alone by a window, or if the weather is nice I practice outside. It's good to take care of distractions ahead of time, so I put away my phone and turn off any music or news that might be on. I take a minute or two to settle into the spot I've chosen, look around, and become comfortable.

Gratitude for My Body

First I focus on my body, feeling the morning energy pulse through me. I feel gratitude for my body and its many parts—my head, my limbs and spine, my muscles, the soft places and the organs within. My body is not perfect, but it holds me, it is my being on this earth.

I am filled with gratitude to the Holy One for this gift.

Gratitude for the Natural World

I look around me at the cactus plant, the branch of a tree, the seed on the ground, the sky above, the grass on the hillside, the tiny ant crawling over my foot, the bird overhead. I become aware of the pulsing of all life around me and focus on this natural world in which we live.

I breathe it in and breathe out my great gratitude for the gift of the natural world.

Gratitude for Ongoing Creation

All the earth is constantly changing. I look at the sky and see the sun now up after the night's darkness. The plant that is a hairsbreadth bigger today than yesterday. The clouds that are moving over me, darkening the light for a moment. The tree that is beginning to bud. And the bruise on my arm that is beginning to heal.

I praise this re-creation of all living beings, and dwell with it and am present with it for a while, grateful for this gift of ongoing creation.

Gratitude for Divine Love

I breathe deeply, open my heart, and acknowledge the love I receive: The touch of a loved one, the kindness of strangers, the beauty all around, the support and strength to move into the day, the breath of the Divine. I let myself feel this love. And I become aware of the love I feel for those close to me, for those I hardly know, for those beyond my reach.

I am filled with gratitude for the flow of love through all being.

Acknowledging the Oneness of All Being

All these gifts I receive, they are one, coming from the Source of All Life. Everything is connected in a fundamental way. I say the words of the central Jewish prayer, the *Sh'ma*, slowly and let them resonate through me: *Sh'ma Yisrael, Adonai Eloheinu, Adonai Ehad* (Listen, Israel. Adonai is our God. Adonai is One). The words on my lips go beyond me, into the world.

I let myself vibrate with their rhythm and beauty.

Giving Back

Because I receive so many gifts beyond measure, I have the responsibility to give back to others. I become conscious of what I need to do in this day ahead: Caring for those around me, mentoring those who come for wisdom, contributing my time and energy to heal and repair the world, living in a more conscious way, honoring the earth.

I set my intention, my *kavvanah*, for the day and commit myself to do the best I can.

Personal Prayer

Finally, I move into my time of personal prayer. I open my heart to the Divine One and say my truth. I name what there is to be named: my sadness and fear, my appreciation and joy, my desire for strength, my gratitude for all the gifts I receive, my need for help in doing what I intend to do.

And then, when I am finished with praying all this, my mind becomes still.

The breath in, the breath out.

The breath in, the breath out.

When I am ready, I move into my day.

Jewish Meditation Resource Guide for Beginning Meditators

Centers of Jewish Meditation

Awakened Heart Project*
Website: www.awakenedheartproject.org

Chochmat HaLev
2215 Prince Street
Berkeley, CA 94705
Phone: (510) 704-9687; Fax: (510) 704-1767
Website: www.chochmat.org
E-mail: info@chochmat.org

Institute for Jewish Spirituality
330 Seventh Avenue, Suite 1902
New York, NY 10001
Phone: (212) 774-3608; Fax: (212) 213-2233
Website: www.ijs-online.org
E-mail: pat@ijs-online.org

Isabella Freedman Jewish Retreat Center / Elat Chayyim
116 Johnson Road
Falls Village, CT 06031
Phone: (800) 398-2630
Website: www.isabellafreedman.org

*No street address.

Jewish Meditation Center of Brooklyn
Weekly meditation at:
Hannah Senesh School
342 Smith Street
Brooklyn, NJ 11231
Mailing address:
25 Broadway, Suite 1700-Bikkurim
New York, NY 10004
Phone: (347) 928-4562
Website: www.jmcbrooklyn.org
E-mail: info@jmcbrooklyn.org

Makor Or*
P. O. Box 590418
San Francisco, CA 94159
Website: www.nishmathayyim.org/teachers.php

Metivta: A Center for Contemplative Judaism
10880 Wilshire Boulevard, Suite 920
Los Angeles, CA 90024
Phone: (818) 654-9293
Website: www.metivta.org
E-mail: metivta@metivta.org

Nishmat Hayyim
1320 Centre Street, Suite 306
Newton, MA 02459
Phone: (617) 244-3757
Website: www.nishmathayyim.org/teachers.php
E-mail: office@nishmathayyim.org

*No street address.

Selected Books on Jewish Meditation and Kabbalah

Addison, Howard A. *Cast in God's Image: Discover Your Personality Type Using the Enneagram and Kabbalah.* Woodstock, Vt.: Jewish Lights, 2001.

———. *The Enneagram and Kabbalah: Reading Your Soul.* 2nd ed. Woodstock, Vt.: Jewish Lights, 2006.

Ariel, David. *Kabbalah: The Mystic Quest in Judaism.* Lanham, MD: Rowman & Littlefield, 2005.

Besserman, Perle. *Kabbalah and Jewish Mysticism.* Boston: Shambhala, 1997.

Boorstein, Sylvia. *That's Funny, You Don't Look Buddhist: On Being a Faithful Jew and a Passionate Buddhist.* San Francisco: HarperSanFrancisco, 1997.

Cooper, David A. *Three Gates to Meditation Practice: A Personal Journey into Sufism, Buddhism, and Judaism.* Woodstock, Vt.; SkyLight Paths, 2000.

———. *God Is a Verb: Kabbalah and the Practice of Mystical Judaism.* New York: Riverhead Books, 1997.

———. *A Heart of Stillness: A Complete Guide to Learning the Art of Meditation.* Woodstock, Vt.: SkyLight Paths, 1999.

———. *Silence, Simplicity & Solitude: A Complete Guide to Spiritual Retreat at Home.* Woodstock, Vt.: SkyLight Paths, 1999.

Davis, Avram, ed. *Meditation from the Heart of Judaism: Today's Teachers Share Their Practices, Techniques, and Faith.* Woodstock, Vt.: Jewish Lights, 1999.

Davis, Avram. *The Way of Flame: A Guide to the Forgotten Mystical Tradition of Jewish Meditation.* Woodstock, Vt.: Jewish Lights, 1999.

Davis, Avram, and Manuela Dunn-Mascetti. *Judaic Mysticism.* New York: Hyperion, 1997.

Fisdel, Steven A. *Practice of Kabbalah: Meditation in Judaism.* Northvale, N.J.: Jason Aronson, 1996.

Frankiel, Tamar. *Kabbalah: A Brief Introduction for Christians.* Woodstock, Vt.: Jewish Lights, 2006.

———. *The Gift of Kabbalah: Discovering the Secrets of Heaven, Renewing Your Life on Earth.* Woodstock, Vt.: Jewish Lights, 2003.

Frankiel, Tamar, and Judy Greenfeld. *Entering the Temple of Dreams: Jewish Prayers, Movements, and Meditations for the End of the Day*. Woodstock, Vt.; Jewish Lights, 2000.

———. *Minding the Temple of the Soul: Balancing Body, Mind, and Spirit through Traditional Jewish Prayer, Movement and Meditation*. Woodstock, Vt.: Jewish Lights, 1997.

Hoffman, Edward. *The Way of Splendor: Jewish Mysticism and Modern Psychology.* Up. ed. Lanham, MD: Rowman & Littlefield, 2006.

———. *The Heavenly Ladder: Kabbalistic Techniques for Inner Growth.* 2nd ed. London: Prism Press, 1996.

Kaplan, Aryeh. *Jewish Meditation: A Practical Guide.* New York: Schocken Books, 1985.

———. *Meditation and Kabbalah.* Northvale, N.J.: Jason Aronson, 1995.

Kushner, Lawrence. *Honey from the Rock: An Easy Introduction to Jewish Mysticism.* Woodstock, Vt.: Jewish Lights, 2000.

Labowitz, Shoni. *Miraculous Living: A Guided Journey in Kabbalah Through the Ten Gates of the Tree of Life.* New York: Simon and Schuster: 1998.

Matt, Daniel C. *The Essential Kabbalah: The Heart of Jewish Mysticism.* San Francisco: HarperSanFrancisco, 1996.

———. *Zohar: The Book of Enlightenment.* Ramsey, N.J.: Paulist Press, 1983.

Michaelson, Jay. *God in Your Body: Kabbalah, Mindfulness and Embodied Spiritual Practice.* Woodstock, Vt.: Jewish Lights, 2006.

Ribner, Melinda. *Everyday Kabbalah: A Practical Guide to Jewish Meditation, Healing, and Personal Growth.* Secaucus, N.J.: Citadel Press, 1998.

Roth, Jeff. *Jewish Meditation Practices for Everyday Life: Awakening Your Heart, Connecting with God*. Woodstock, Vt.: Jewish Lights, 2009.

Shapira, Kalonymus Kalman. *Conscious Community: A Guide to Inner Work*. Northvale, N.J.: Jason Aronson, 2004.

Steinsaltz, Adin. *The Thirteen Petalled Rose: A Discourse on the Essence of Jewish Existence & Belief*. New York: Basic Books, 2006.

Verman, Mark. *The History and Varieties of Jewish Meditation*. Northvale, N.J.: Jason Aronson, 1996.

Selected Books on the Jewish Spiritual Path

Buxbaum, Yitzhak. *Jewish Spiritual Practices*. Northvale, N.J.: Jason Aronson, 1990.

Dosick, Wayne. *Soul Judaism: Dancing with God into a New Era*. Woodstock, Vt.: Jewish Lights, 1999.

Green, Arthur. *These Are the Words: A Vocabulary of Jewish Spiritual Life*. Woodstock, Vt.: Jewish Lights, 2000.

Kula, Irwin and Vanessa L. Ochs, eds. *The Book of Jewish Sacred Practices: CLAL's Guide to Everyday & Holiday Rituals & Blessings*. Woodstock, Vt.: Jewish Lights, 2001.

Kushner, Lawrence. *The River of Light: Jewish Mystical Awareness*. Woodstock, Vt.: Jewish Lights, 2000.

———. *God Was in This Place & I, i Did Not Know: Finding Self, Spirituality and Ultimate Meaning*. Woodstock, Vt.: Jewish Lights, 1993.

Mirel, James L., and Karen Bonnell Werth. *Stepping Stones to Jewish Spiritual Living: Walking the Path Morning, Noon, and Night*. Woodstock, Vt.: Jewish Lights, 2000.

Shapiro, Rami M. *Minyan: Ten Principles for Living a Life of Integrity*. New York: Bell Tower, 1997.

Strassfeld, Michael. *A Book of Life: Embracing Judaism as a Spiritual Practice*. Woodstock, Vt.: Jewish Lights, 2006.

Umansky, Ellen M., and Dianne Ashton. *Four Centuries of Jewish Women's Spirituality: A Sourcebook.* Rev. ed. Lebanon, N.H.: Brandeis University Press, 2009.

Selected Books on *Shabbat*

Bernhard, Durga Yael. *Around the World in One Shabbat: Jewish People Celebrate the Sabbath Together*. Woodstock, Vt.: Jewish Lights, 2011.

Cooper, David A. *The Handbook of Jewish Meditation Practices: A Guide for Enriching the Sabbath and Other Days of Your Life.* Woodstock, Vt.: Jewish Lights, 2000.

Heschel, Abraham Joshua. *The Sabbath.* New York: Farrar, Straus & Giroux, 2005.

Mykoff, Moshe. *Seventh Heaven: Celebrating Shabbat with Rebbe Nachman of Breslov*. With the Breslov Research Institute. Woodstock, Vt.: Jewish Lights, 2003.

Wolfson, Ron. *Shabbat: The Family Guide to Preparing for and Celebrating the Sabbath*. 2nd ed. Woodstock, Vt.: Jewish Lights, 2002.

Selected Books on Jewish Holidays

Adelman, Penina V. *Miriam's Well: Rituals for Jewish Women Around the Year.* 2nd ed. New York: Biblio Press, 1990.

Klagsbrun, Francine. *Jewish Days: A Book of Jewish Life and Culture Around the Year.* New York: Noonday Press, 1996.

Milgram, Goldie. *Reclaiming Judaism as a Spiritual Practice: Holy Days and Shabbat*. Woodstock, Vt.: Jewish Lights, 2004.

Olitzky, Kerry M., and Daniel Judson, eds. *The Rituals & Practices of a Jewish Life: A Handbook for Personal Spiritual Renewal*. Woodstock, Vt.: Jewish Lights, 2002.

Strassfeld, Michael. *The Jewish Holidays: A Guide and Commentary.* New York: Quill, 2001.

Waskow, Arthur. *Seasons of Our Joy: A Modern Guide to the Jewish Holidays.* Boston: Beacon, 1990.

Selected Books for the Study of Torah

Cohen, Norman J. *The Way Into Torah.* Woodstock, Vt.: Jewish Lights, 2000.

Frankel, Ellen. *The Five Books of Miriam: A Woman's Commentary on the Torah.* New York: HarperCollins, 1998.

Goldstein, Elyse, ed. *The Women's Torah Commentary: New Insights from Women Rabbis on the 54 Weekly Torah Portions.* Woodstock, Vt.: Jewish Lights, 2008.

Salkin, Jeffrey K., ed. *The Modern Men's Torah Commentary: New Insights from Jewish Men on the 54 Weekly Torah Portions.* Woodstock, Vt.: Jewish Lights, 2009.

Zornberg, Avivah Gottlieb. *The Beginning of Desire: Reflections on Genesis.* New York: Schocken Books, 2011.

Selected Books on Jewish Prayer

Comins, Mike. *Making Prayer Real: Leading Jewish Spiritual Voices on Why Prayer Is Difficult and What to Do about It.* Woodstock, Vt.: Jewish Lights, 2010.

Donin, Hayim Halevy. *To Pray As a Jew: A Guide to the Prayer Book and the Synagogue Service.* New York: Basic Books, 1980.

Garfiel, Evelyn. *Service of the Heart: A Guide to the Jewish Prayer Book.* Northvale, N.J.: Jason Aronson, 1994.

Green, Arthur and Barry W. Holtz. *Your Word Is Fire: The Hasidic Masters on Contemplative Prayer.* Woodstock, Vt.: Jewish Lights, 1993.

Hammer, Reuven. *Entering Jewish Prayer: A Guide to Personal Devotion and the Worship Service.* New York: Schocken Books, 1994.

Hoffman, Lawrence, ed. *My People's Prayer Book: Traditional Prayers, Modern Commentaries.* 10 vols. Woodstock, Vt.: Jewish Lights, 1997–2007.

Hoffman, Lawrence A. *The Way Into Jewish Prayer.* Woodstock, Vt.: Jewish Lights, 2000.

Selected Books on Blessings

Grishaver, Joel Lurie. *And You Shall Be a Blessing: An Unfolding of the Six Words That Begin Every Brakhah.* Northvale, N.J.: Jason Aronson, 1993.

Olitzky, Kerry M. *Life's Daily Blessings: Inspiring Reflections on Gratitude and Joy for Every Day, Based on Jewish Wisdom.* Woodstock, Vt.: Jewish Lights, 2009.

———. *100 Blessings Every Day: Daily Twelve Step Recovery Affirmations, Exercises for Personal Growth & Renewal Reflecting Seasons of the Jewish Year.* Woodstock, Vt.: Jewish Lights, 1993.

Prager, Marcia. *The Path of Blessing: Experiencing the Energy and Abundance of the Divine.* Woodstock, Vt.: Jewish Lights, 2003.

Selected Books on *Mitzvot*

Biale, Rachel. *Women and Jewish Law: The Essential Texts, Their History, and Their Relevance for Today.* New York: Schocken Books, 1995.

Bonder, Nilton. *The Kabbalah of Money: Jewish Insights on Giving, Owning, and Receiving*. Boston: Shambhala, 1996.
Donin, Hayim Halevy. *To Be a Jew: A Guide to Jewish Observance in Contemporary Life*. New York: Basic Books, 1972.
Milgram, Goldie. *Meaning & Mitzvah: Daily Practices for Reclaiming Judaism through Prayer, God, Torah, Hebrew, Mitzvot and Peoplehood*. Woodstock, Vt.: Jewish Lights, 2005.
Waskow, Arthur. *Down-to-Earth Judaism: Food, Money, Sex, and the Rest of Life*. New York: William Morrow & Co., 1995.

Selected Books on *Tikkun Olam*

Bernstein, Ellen, ed. *Ecology & the Jewish Spirit: Where Nature & the Sacred Meet*. Woodstock, Vt.: Jewish Lights, 2000.
Dorff, Elliot N. *The Way Into Tikkun Olam (Repairing the World)*. Woodstock, Vt.: Jewish Lights, 2007.
Gottlieb, Lynn. *She Who Dwells Within: A Feminist Vision of a Renewed Judaism*. New York: HarperCollins, 1995.
Jacobs, Jill. *There Shall Be No Needy: Pursuing Social Justice through Jewish Law and Tradition*. Woodstock, Vt.: Jewish Lights, 2010.
———. *Where Justice Dwells: A Hands-on Guide to Doing Social Justice in Your Jewish Community*. Woodstock, Vt.: Jewish Lights, 2011.
Lerner, Michael. *Jewish Renewal: A Path to Healing and Transformation*. New York: G. P. Putnam's Sons, 1994.
Schulweis, Harold M. *Conscience: The Duty to Obey and the Duty to Disobey*. Woodstock, Vt.: Jewish Lights, 2010.
Waskow, Arthur. *Godwrestling—Round 2: Ancient Wisdom, Future Paths.* Woodstock, Vt.: Jewish Lights, 1998.
Weiss, Avraham. *Spiritual Activism: A Jewish Guide to Leadership and Repairing the World*. Woodstock, Vt.: Jewish Lights, 2010.

Theology/Philosophy/The Way Into... Series

The Way Into... series offers an accessible and highly usable "guided tour" of the Jewish faith, people, history and beliefs—in total, an introduction to Judaism that will enable you to understand and interact with the sacred texts of the Jewish tradition. Each volume is written by a leading contemporary scholar and teacher, and explores one key aspect of Judaism. The Way Into... series enables all readers to achieve a real sense of Jewish cultural literacy through guided study.

The Way Into Encountering God in Judaism
By Rabbi Neil Gillman, PhD
For everyone who wants to understand how Jews have encountered God throughout history and today.
6 x 9, 240 pp, Quality PB, 978-1-58023-199-2 **$18.99**; HC, 978-1-58023-025-4 **$21.95**

Also Available: **The Jewish Approach to God:** A Brief Introduction for Christians
By Rabbi Neil Gillman, PhD
5½ x 8½, 192 pp, Quality PB, 978-1-58023-190-9 **$16.95**

The Way Into Jewish Mystical Tradition
By Rabbi Lawrence Kushner
Allows readers to interact directly with the sacred mystical texts of the Jewish tradition. An accessible introduction to the concepts of Jewish mysticism, their religious and spiritual significance, and how they relate to life today.
6 x 9, 224 pp, Quality PB, 978-1-58023-200-5 **$18.99**; HC, 978-1-58023-029-2 **$21.95**

The Way Into Jewish Prayer
By Rabbi Lawrence A. Hoffman, PhD
Opens the door to 3,000 years of Jewish prayer, making anyone feel at home in the Jewish way of communicating with God.
6 x 9, 208 pp, Quality PB, 978-1-58023-201-2 **$18.99**

The Way Into Jewish Prayer Teacher's Guide
By Rabbi Jennifer Ossakow Goldsmith
8½ x 11, 42 pp, PB, 978-1-58023-345-3 **$8.99**
Download a free copy at www.jewishlights.com.

The Way Into Judaism and the Environment
By Jeremy Benstein, PhD
Explores the ways in which Judaism contributes to contemporary social-environmental issues, the extent to which Judaism is part of the problem and how it can be part of the solution.
6 x 9, 288 pp, Quality PB, 978-1-58023-368-2 **$18.99**

The Way Into *Tikkun Olam* (Repairing the World)
By Rabbi Elliot N. Dorff, PhD
An accessible introduction to the Jewish concept of the individual's responsibility to care for others and repair the world.
6 x 9, 304 pp, Quality PB, 978-1-58023-328-6 **$18.99**

The Way Into Torah
By Rabbi Norman J. Cohen, PhD
Helps guide you in the exploration of the origins and development of Torah, explains why it should be studied and how to do it.
6 x 9, 176 pp, Quality PB, 978-1-58023-198-5 **$16.99**

The Way Into the Varieties of Jewishness
By Sylvia Barack Fishman, PhD
Explores the religious and historical understanding of what it has meant to be Jewish from ancient times to the present controversy over "Who is a Jew?"
6 x 9, 288 pp, Quality PB, 978-1-58023-367-5 **$18.99**; HC, 978-1-58023-030-8 **$24.99**

Life Cycle

Marriage/Parenting/Family/Aging

The New Jewish Baby Album: Creating and Celebrating the Beginning of a Spiritual Life—A Jewish Lights Companion
By the Editors at Jewish Lights; Foreword by Anita Diamant; Preface by Rabbi Sandy Eisenberg Sasso
A spiritual keepsake that will be treasured for generations. More than just a memory book, *shows you how—and why it's important*—to create a Jewish home and a Jewish life. 8 x 10, 64 pp, Deluxe Padded HC, Full-color illus., 978-1-58023-138-1 **$19.95**

The Jewish Pregnancy Book: A Resource for the Soul, Body & Mind during Pregnancy, Birth & the First Three Months *By Sandy Falk, MD, and Rabbi Daniel Judson, with Steven A. Rapp* Medical information, prayers and rituals for each stage of pregnancy. 7 x 10, 208 pp, b/w photos, Quality PB, 978-1-58023-178-7 **$16.95**

Celebrating Your New Jewish Daughter: Creating Jewish Ways to Welcome Baby Girls into the Covenant—New and Traditional Ceremonies *By Debra Nussbaum Cohen; Foreword by Rabbi Sandy Eisenberg Sasso* 6 x 9, 272 pp, Quality PB, 978-1-58023-090-2 **$18.95**

The New Jewish Baby Book, 2nd Edition: Names, Ceremonies & Customs—A Guide for Today's Families *By Anita Diamant* 6 x 9, 320 pp, Quality PB, 978-1-58023-251-7 **$19.99**

Parenting as a Spiritual Journey: Deepening Ordinary and Extraordinary Events into Sacred Occasions *By Rabbi Nancy Fuchs-Kreimer, PhD*
6 x 9, 224 pp, Quality PB, 978-1-58023-016-2 **$17.99**

Parenting Jewish Teens: A Guide for the Perplexed
By Joanne Doades Explores the questions and issues that shape the world in which today's Jewish teenagers live and offers constructive advice to parents.
6 x 9, 176 pp, Quality PB, 978-1-58023-305-7 **$16.99**

Judaism for Two: A Spiritual Guide for Strengthening and Celebrating Your Loving Relationship *By Rabbi Nancy Fuchs-Kreimer, PhD, and Rabbi Nancy H. Wiener, DMin; Foreword by Rabbi Elliot N. Dorff, PhD*
Addresses the ways Jewish teachings can enhance and strengthen committed relationships. 6 x 9, 224 pp, Quality PB, 978-1-58023-254-8 **$16.99**

The Creative Jewish Wedding Book, 2nd Edition: A Hands-On Guide to New & Old Traditions, Ceremonies & Celebrations *By Gabrielle Kaplan-Mayer*
9 x 9, 288 pp, b/w photos, Quality PB, 978-1-58023-398-9 **$19.99**

Divorce Is a Mitzvah: A Practical Guide to Finding Wholeness and Holiness When Your Marriage Dies *By Rabbi Perry Netter; Afterword by Rabbi Laura Geller*
6 x 9, 224 pp, Quality PB, 978-1-58023-172-5 **$16.95**

Embracing the Covenant: Converts to Judaism Talk About Why & How
By Rabbi Allan Berkowitz and Patti Moskovitz 6 x 9, 192 pp, Quality PB, 978-1-879045-50-7 **$16.95**

The Guide to Jewish Interfaith Family Life: An InterfaithFamily.com Handbook
Edited by Ronnie Friedland and Edmund Case
6 x 9, 384 pp, Quality PB, 978-1-58023-153-4 **$18.95**

A Heart of Wisdom: Making the Jewish Journey from Midlife through the Elder Years
Edited by Susan Berrin; Foreword by Rabbi Harold Kushner
6 x 9, 384 pp, Quality PB, 978-1-58023-051-3 **$18.95**

Introducing My Faith and My Community: The Jewish Outreach Institute Guide for the Christian in a Jewish Interfaith Relationship
By Rabbi Kerry M. Olitzky 6 x 9, 176 pp, Quality PB, 978-1-58023-192-3 **$16.99**

Making a Successful Jewish Interfaith Marriage: The Jewish Outreach Institute Guide to Opportunities, Challenges and Resources *By Rabbi Kerry M. Olitzky with Joan Peterson Littman*
6 x 9, 176 pp, Quality PB, 978-1-58023-170-1 **$16.95**

A Man's Responsibility: A Jewish Guide to Being a Son, a Partner in Marriage, a Father and a Community Leader *By Rabbi Joseph B. Meszler*
6 x 9, 192 pp, Quality PB, 978-1-58023-435-1 **$16.99**; HC, 978-1-58023-362-0 **$21.99**

So That Your Values Live On: Ethical Wills and How to Prepare Them
Edited by Rabbi Jack Riemer and Rabbi Nathaniel Stampfer
6 x 9, 272 pp, Quality PB, 978-1-879045-34-7 **$18.99**

Holidays/Holy Days

Who by Fire, Who by Water—*Un'taneh Tokef*

Edited by Rabbi Lawrence A. Hoffman, PhD

Examines the prayer's theology, authorship and poetry through a set of lively essays, all written in accessible language.

6 x 9, 272 pp, HC, 978-1-58023-424-5 **$24.99**

All These Vows—*Kol Nidre*

Edited by Rabbi Lawrence A. Hoffman, PhD

The most memorable prayer of the Jewish New Year—what it means, why we sing it, and the secret of its magical appeal.

6 x 9, 288 pp, HC, 978-1-58023-430-6 **$24.99**

Rosh Hashanah Readings: Inspiration, Information and Contemplation

Yom Kippur Readings: Inspiration, Information and Contemplation

Edited by Rabbi Dov Peretz Elkins; Section Introductions from Arthur Green's These Are the Words

Rosh Hashanah: 6 x 9, 400 pp, Quality PB, 978-1-58023-437-5 **$19.99**; HC, 978-1-58023-239-5 **$24.99**

Yom Kippur: 6 x 9, 368 pp, Quality PB, 978-1-58023-438-2 **$19.99**; HC, 978-1-58023-271-5 **$24.99**

Jewish Holidays: A Brief Introduction for Christians

By Rabbi Kerry M. Olitzky and Rabbi Daniel Judson

5½ x 8½, 176 pp, Quality PB, 978-1-58023-302-6 **$16.99**

Reclaiming Judaism as a Spiritual Practice: Holy Days and Shabbat

By Rabbi Goldie Milgram 7 x 9, 272 pp, Quality PB, 978-1-58023-205-0 **$19.99**

Shabbat, 2nd Edition: The Family Guide to Preparing for and Celebrating the Sabbath

By Dr. Ron Wolfson 7 x 9, 320 pp, Illus., Quality PB, 978-1-58023-164-0 **$19.99**

Hanukkah, 2nd Edition: The Family Guide to Spiritual Celebration

By Dr. Ron Wolfson 7 x 9, 240 pp, Illus., Quality PB, 978-1-58023-122-0 **$18.95**

The Jewish Family Fun Book, 2nd Edition

Holiday Projects, Everyday Activities, and Travel Ideas with Jewish Themes

By Danielle Dardashti and Roni Sarig; Illus. by Avi Katz

6 x 9, 304 pp, 70+ b/w illus. & diagrams, Quality PB, 978-1-58023-333-0 **$18.99**

Passover

My People's Passover Haggadah

Traditional Texts, Modern Commentaries

Edited by Rabbi Lawrence A. Hoffman, PhD, and David Arnow, PhD

A diverse and exciting collection of commentaries on the traditional Passover Haggadah—in two volumes!

Vol. 1: 7 x 10, 304 pp, HC, 978-1-58023-354-5 **$24.99**

Vol. 2: 7 x 10, 320 pp, HC, 978-1-58023-346-0 **$24.99**

Freedom Journeys: The Tale of Exodus and Wilderness across Millennia

By Rabbi Arthur O. Waskow and Rabbi Phyllis O. Berman

Explores how the story of Exodus echoes in our own time, calling us to relearn and rethink the Passover story through social-justice, ecological, feminist and interfaith perspectives. 6 x 9, 288 pp, HC, 978-1-58023-445-0 **$24.99**

Leading the Passover Journey: The Seder's Meaning Revealed, the Haggadah's Story Retold *By Rabbi Nathan Laufer*

Uncovers the hidden meaning of the Seder's rituals and customs.

6 x 9, 224 pp, Quality PB, 978-1-58023-399-6 **$18.99**; HC, 978-1-58023-211-1 **$24.99**

Creating Lively Passover Seders, 2nd Edition: A Sourcebook of Engaging Tales, Texts & Activities *By David Arnow, PhD* 7 x 9, 464 pp, Quality PB, 978-1-58023-444-3 **$24.99**

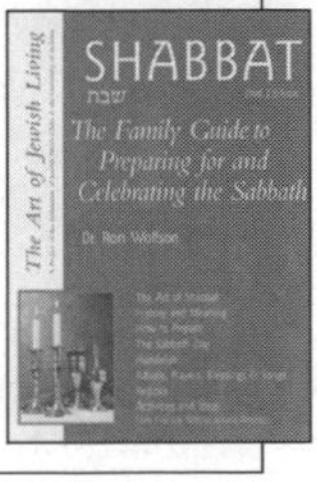

Passover, 2nd Edition: The Family Guide to Spiritual Celebration

By Dr. Ron Wolfson with Joel Lurie Grishaver 7 x 9, 416 pp, Quality PB, 978-1-58023-174-9 **$19.95**

The Women's Passover Companion: Women's Reflections on the Festival of Freedom

Edited by Rabbi Sharon Cohen Anisfeld, Tara Mohr and Catherine Spector; Foreword by Paula E. Hyman

6 x 9, 352 pp, Quality PB, 978-1-58023-231-9 **$19.99**; HC, 978-1-58023-128-2 **$24.95**

The Women's Seder Sourcebook: Rituals & Readings for Use at the Passover Seder

Edited by Rabbi Sharon Cohen Anisfeld, Tara Mohr and Catherine Spector

6 x 9, 384 pp, Quality PB, 978-1-58023-232-6 **$19.99**

Ecology/Environment

A Wild Faith: Jewish Ways into Wilderness, Wilderness Ways into Judaism
By Rabbi Mike Comins; Foreword by Nigel Savage 6 x 9, 240 pp, Quality PB, 978-1-58023-316-3 **$16.99**

Ecology & the Jewish Spirit: Where Nature & the Sacred Meet
Edited by Ellen Bernstein 6 x 9, 288 pp, Quality PB, 978-1-58023-082-7 **$18.99**

Torah of the Earth: Exploring 4,000 Years of Ecology in Jewish Thought
Vol. 1: Biblical Israel & Rabbinic Judaism; Vol. 2: Zionism & Eco-Judaism
Edited by Rabbi Arthur Waskow Vol. 1: 6 x 9, 272 pp, Quality PB, 978-1-58023-086-5 **$19.95**
Vol. 2: 6 x 9, 336 pp, Quality PB, 978-1-58023-087-2 **$19.95**

The Way Into Judaism and the Environment *By Jeremy Benstein, PhD*
6 x 9, 288 pp, Quality PB, 978-1-58023-368-2 **$18.99**; HC, 978-1-58023-268-5 **$24.99**

Graphic Novels/History

The Adventures of Rabbi Harvey: A Graphic Novel of Jewish Wisdom and Wit in the Wild West *By Steve Sheinkin* 6 x 9, 144 pp, Full-color illus., Quality PB, 978-1-58023-310-1 **$16.99**

Rabbi Harvey Rides Again: A Graphic Novel of Jewish Folktales Let Loose in the Wild West *By Steve Sheinkin* 6 x 9, 144 pp, Full-color illus., Quality PB, 978-1-58023-347-7 **$16.99**

Rabbi Harvey vs. the Wisdom Kid: A Graphic Novel of Dueling Jewish Folktales in the Wild West *By Steve Sheinkin*
Rabbi Harvey's first book-length adventure—and toughest challenge.
6 x 9, 144 pp, Full-color illus., Quality PB, 978-1-58023-422-1 **$16.99**

The Story of the Jews: A 4,000-Year Adventure—A Graphic History Book
By Stan Mack 6 x 9, 288 pp, Illus., Quality PB, 978-1-58023-155-8 **$16.99**

Grief/Healing

Facing Illness, Finding God: How Judaism Can Help You and Caregivers Cope When Body or Spirit Fails *By Rabbi Joseph B. Meszler*
Will help you find spiritual strength for healing amid the fear, pain and chaos of illness. 6 x 9, 208 pp, Quality PB, 978-1-58023-423-8 **$16.99**

Midrash & Medicine: Healing Body and Soul in the Jewish Interpretive Tradition *Edited by Rabbi William Cutter, PhD; Foreword by Michele F. Prince, LCSW, MAJCS*
Explores how midrash can help you see beyond the physical aspects of healing to tune in to your spiritual source.
6 x 9, 352 pp, Quality PB, 978-1-58023-484-9 **$21.99**; HC, 978-1-58023-428-3 **$29.99**

Healing from Despair: Choosing Wholeness in a Broken World
By Rabbi Elie Kaplan Spitz with Erica Shapiro Taylor; Foreword by Abraham J. Twerski, MD
5½ x 8½, 208 pp, Quality PB, 978-1-58023-436-8 **$16.99**

Healing and the Jewish Imagination: Spiritual and Practical Perspectives on Judaism and Health *Edited by Rabbi William Cutter, PhD*
6 x 9, 240 pp, Quality PB, 978-1-58023-373-6 **$19.99**

Grief in Our Seasons: A Mourner's Kaddish Companion *By Rabbi Kerry M. Olitzky*
4½ x 6½, 448 pp, Quality PB, 978-1-879045-55-2 **$15.95**

Healing of Soul, Healing of Body: Spiritual Leaders Unfold the Strength & Solace in Psalms *Edited by Rabbi Simkha Y. Weintraub, LCSW*
6 x 9, 128 pp, 2-color illus. text, Quality PB, 978-1-879045-31-6 **$16.99**

Mourning & Mitzvah, 2nd Edition: A Guided Journal for Walking the Mourner's Path through Grief to Healing *By Rabbi Anne Brener, LCSW*
7½ x 9, 304 pp, Quality PB, 978-1-58023-113-8 **$19.99**

Tears of Sorrow, Seeds of Hope, 2nd Edition: A Jewish Spiritual Companion for Infertility and Pregnancy Loss *By Rabbi Nina Beth Cardin*
6 x 9, 208 pp, Quality PB, 978-1-58023-233-3 **$18.99**

A Time to Mourn, a Time to Comfort, 2nd Edition: A Guide to Jewish Bereavement *By Dr. Ron Wolfson; Foreword by Rabbi David J. Wolpe*
7 x 9, 384 pp, Quality PB, 978-1-58023-253-1 **$21.99**

When a Grandparent Dies: A Kid's Own Remembering Workbook for Dealing with Shiva and the Year Beyond *By Nechama Liss-Levinson, PhD*
8 x 10, 48 pp, 2-color text, HC, 978-1-879045-44-6 **$15.95** *For ages 7–13*

Spirituality/Prayer

Making Prayer Real: Leading Jewish Spiritual Voices on Why Prayer Is Difficult and What to Do about It *By Rabbi Mike Comins*
A new and different response to the challenges of Jewish prayer, with "best prayer practices" from Jewish spiritual leaders of all denominations.
6 x 9, 320 pp, Quality PB, 978-1-58023-417-7 **$18.99**

Witnesses to the One: The Spiritual History of the *Sh'ma*
By Rabbi Joseph B. Meszler; Foreword by Rabbi Elyse Goldstein
6 x 9, 176 pp, Quality PB, 978-1-58023-400-9 **$16.99**; HC, 978-1-58023-309-5 **$19.99**

My People's Prayer Book Series: Traditional Prayers, Modern Commentaries *Edited by Rabbi Lawrence A. Hoffman, PhD*
Provides diverse and exciting commentary to the traditional liturgy. Will help you find new wisdom in Jewish prayer, and bring liturgy into your life. Each book includes Hebrew text, modern translations and commentaries from all perspectives of the Jewish world.

Vol. 1—The *Sh'ma* and Its Blessings
7 x 10, 168 pp, HC, 978-1-879045-79-8 **$29.99**
Vol. 2—The *Amidah* 7 x 10, 240 pp, HC, 978-1-879045-80-4 **$24.95**
Vol. 3—*P'sukei D'zimrah* (Morning Psalms)
7 x 10, 240 pp, HC, 978-1-879045-81-1 **$29.99**
Vol. 4—*Seder K'riat Hatorah* (The Torah Service)
7 x 10, 264 pp, HC, 978-1-879045-82-8 **$29.99**
Vol. 5—*Birkhot Hashachar* (Morning Blessings)
7 x 10, 240 pp, HC, 978-1-879045-83-5 **$24.95**
Vol. 6—*Tachanun* and Concluding Prayers
7 x 10, 240 pp, HC, 978-1-879045-84-2 **$24.95**
Vol. 7—Shabbat at Home 7 x 10, 240 pp, HC, 978-1-879045-85-9 **$24.95**
Vol. 8—*Kabbalat Shabbat* (Welcoming Shabbat in the Synagogue)
7 x 10, 240 pp, HC, 978-1-58023-121-3 **$24.99**
Vol. 9—Welcoming the Night: *Minchah* and *Ma'ariv* (Afternoon and Evening Prayer) 7 x 10, 272 pp, HC, 978-1-58023-262-3 **$24.99**
Vol. 10—Shabbat Morning: *Shacharit* and *Musaf* (Morning and Additional Services) 7 x 10, 240 pp, HC, 978-1-58023-240-1 **$29.99**

Spirituality/Lawrence Kushner

I'm God; You're Not: Observations on Organized Religion & Other Disguises of the Ego
6 x 9, 256 pp, HC, 978-1-58023-441-2 **$21.99**

The Book of Letters: A Mystical Hebrew Alphabet
Popular HC Edition, 6 x 9, 80 pp, 2-color text, 978-1-879045-00-2 **$24.95**
Collector's Limited Edition, 9 x 12, 80 pp, gold-foil-embossed pages, w/ limited-edition silkscreened print, 978-1-879045-04-0 **$349.00**

The Book of Miracles: A Young Person's Guide to Jewish Spiritual Awareness
6 x 9, 96 pp, 2-color illus., HC, 978-1-879045-78-1 **$16.95** *For ages 9–13*

The Book of Words: Talking Spiritual Life, Living Spiritual Talk
6 x 9, 160 pp, Quality PB, 978-1-58023-020-9 **$18.99**

Eyes Remade for Wonder: A Lawrence Kushner Reader *Introduction by Thomas Moore*
6 x 9, 240 pp, Quality PB, 978-1-58023-042-1 **$18.95**

God Was in This Place & I, i Did Not Know: Finding Self, Spirituality and Ultimate Meaning 6 x 9, 192 pp, Quality PB, 978-1-879045-33-0 **$16.95**

Honey from the Rock: An Introduction to Jewish Mysticism
6 x 9, 176 pp, Quality PB, 978-1-58023-073-5 **$16.95**

Invisible Lines of Connection: Sacred Stories of the Ordinary
5½ x 8½, 160 pp, Quality PB, 978-1-879045-98-9 **$15.95**

Jewish Spirituality: A Brief Introduction for Christians
5½ x 8½, 112 pp, Quality PB, 978-1-58023-150-3 **$12.95**

The River of Light: Jewish Mystical Awareness
6 x 9, 192 pp, Quality PB, 978-1-58023-096-4 **$16.95**

The Way Into Jewish Mystical Tradition
6 x 9, 224 pp, Quality PB, 978-1-58023-200-5 **$18.99**; HC, 978-1-58023-029-2 **$21.95**

Spirituality

Repentance: The Meaning and Practice of *Teshuvah*
By Dr. Louis E. Newman; Foreword by Rabbi Harold M. Schulweis; Preface by Rabbi Karyn D. Kedar
Examines both the practical and philosophical dimensions of *teshuvah*, Judaism's core religious-moral teaching on repentance, and its value for us—Jews and non-Jews alike—today. 6 x 9, 256 pp, HC, 978-1-58023-426-9 **$24.99**

***Tanya,* the Masterpiece of Hasidic Wisdom**
Selections Annotated & Explained
Translation & Annotation by Rabbi Rami Shapiro; Foreword by Rabbi Zalman M. Schachter-Shalomi
Brings the genius of *Tanya*, one of the most powerful books of Jewish wisdom, to anyone seeking to deepen their understanding of the soul.
5½ x 8½, 240 pp, Quality PB, 978-1-59473-275-1 **$16.99**
(A book from SkyLight Paths, Jewish Lights' sister imprint)

Aleph-Bet Yoga: Embodying the Hebrew Letters for Physical and Spiritual Well-Being
By Steven A. Rapp; Foreword by Tamar Frankiel, PhD, and Judy Greenfeld; Preface by Hart Lazer
7 x 10, 128 pp, b/w photos, Quality PB, Lay-flat binding, 978-1-58023-162-6 **$16.95**

A Book of Life: Embracing Judaism as a Spiritual Practice
By Rabbi Michael Strassfeld 6 x 9, 544 pp, Quality PB, 978-1-58023-247-0 **$19.99**

Bringing the Psalms to Life: How to Understand and Use the Book of Psalms
By Rabbi Daniel F. Polish, PhD 6 x 9, 208 pp, Quality PB, 978-1-58023-157-2 **$16.95**

Does the Soul Survive? A Jewish Journey to Belief in Afterlife, Past Lives & Living with Purpose *By Rabbi Elie Kaplan Spitz; Foreword by Brian L. Weiss, MD*
6 x 9, 288 pp, Quality PB, 978-1-58023-165-7 **$16.99**

First Steps to a New Jewish Spirit: Reb Zalman's Guide to Recapturing the Intimacy & Ecstasy in Your Relationship with God *By Rabbi Zalman M. Schachter-Shalomi with Donald Gropman* 6 x 9, 144 pp, Quality PB, 978-1-58023-182-4 **$16.95**

Foundations of Sephardic Spirituality: The Inner Life of Jews of the Ottoman Empire
By Rabbi Marc D. Angel, PhD 6 x 9, 224 pp, Quality PB, 978-1-58023-341-5 **$18.99**

God & the Big Bang: Discovering Harmony between Science & Spirituality
By Dr. Daniel C. Matt 6 x 9, 216 pp, Quality PB, 978-1-879045-89-7 **$16.99**

God in Our Relationships: Spirituality between People from the Teachings of Martin Buber *By Rabbi Dennis S. Ross* 5½ x 8½, 160 pp, Quality PB, 978-1-58023-147-3 **$16.95**

The Jewish Lights Spirituality Handbook: A Guide to Understanding, Exploring & Living a Spiritual Life *Edited by Stuart M. Matlins*
What exactly is "Jewish" about spirituality? How do I make it a part of my life? Fifty of today's foremost spiritual leaders share their ideas and experience with us.
6 x 9, 456 pp, Quality PB, 978-1-58023-093-3 **$19.99**

Judaism, Physics and God: Searching for Sacred Metaphors in a Post-Einstein World
By Rabbi David W. Nelson 6 x 9, 352 pp, Quality PB, inc. reader's discussion guide, 978-1-58023-306-4 **$18.99**; HC, 352 pp, 978-1-58023-252-4 **$24.99**

Meaning & Mitzvah: Daily Practices for Reclaiming Judaism through Prayer, God, Torah, Hebrew, Mitzvot and Peoplehood *By Rabbi Goldie Milgram*
7 x 9, 336 pp, Quality PB, 978-1-58023-256-2 **$19.99**

Minding the Temple of the Soul: Balancing Body, Mind, and Spirit through Traditional Jewish Prayer, Movement, and Meditation *By Tamar Frankiel, PhD, and Judy Greenfeld*
7 x 10, 184 pp, Illus., Quality PB, 978-1-879045-64-4 **$18.99**

One God Clapping: The Spiritual Path of a Zen Rabbi *By Rabbi Alan Lew with Sherril Jaffe*
5½ x 8½, 336 pp, Quality PB, 978-1-58023-115-2 **$16.95**

The Soul of the Story: Meetings with Remarkable People
By Rabbi David Zeller 6 x 9, 288 pp, HC, 978-1-58023-272-2 **$21.99**

There Is No Messiah … and You're It: The Stunning Transformation of Judaism's Most Provocative Idea *By Rabbi Robert N. Levine, DD*
6 x 9, 192 pp, Quality PB, 978-1-58023-255-5 **$16.99**

These Are the Words: A Vocabulary of Jewish Spiritual Life
By Rabbi Arthur Green, PhD 6 x 9, 304 pp, Quality PB, 978-1-58023-107-7 **$18.95**

Social Justice

Confronting Scandal
How Jews Can Respond When Jews Do Bad Things
By Dr. Erica Brown
A framework to transform our sense of shame over reports of Jews committing crime into actions that inspire and sustain a moral culture.
6 x 9, 192 pp, HC, 978-1-58023-440-5 **$24.99**

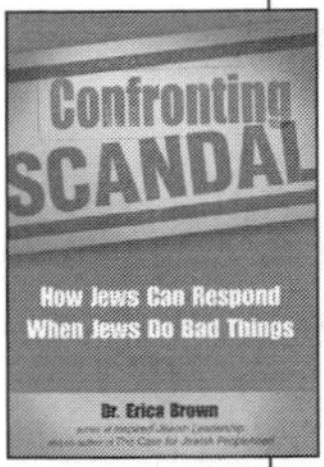

There Shall Be No Needy
Pursuing Social Justice through Jewish Law and Tradition
By Rabbi Jill Jacobs; Foreword by Rabbi Elliot N. Dorff, PhD; Preface by Simon Greer
Confronts the most pressing issues of twenty-first-century America from a deeply Jewish perspective. 6 x 9, 288 pp, Quality PB, 978-1-58023-425-2 **$16.99**

There Shall Be No Needy Teacher's Guide 8½ x 11, 56 pp, PB, 978-1-58023-429-0 **$8.99**

Conscience
The Duty to Obey and the Duty to Disobey
By Rabbi Harold M. Schulweis
Examines the idea of conscience and the role conscience plays in our relationships to government, law, ethics, religion, human nature, God—and to each other.
6 x 9, 160 pp, Quality PB, 978-1-58023-419-1 **$16.99**; HC, 978-1-58023-375-0 **$19.99**

Judaism and Justice
The Jewish Passion to Repair the World
By Rabbi Sidney Schwarz; Foreword by Ruth Messinger
Explores the relationship between Judaism, social justice and the Jewish identity of American Jews. 6 x 9, 352 pp, Quality PB, 978-1-58023-353-8 **$19.99**

Spirituality/Women's Interest

New Jewish Feminism
Probing the Past, Forging the Future
Edited by Rabbi Elyse Goldstein; Foreword by Anita Diamant
Looks at the growth and accomplishments of Jewish feminism and what they mean for Jewish women today and tomorrow.
6 x 9, 480 pp, Quality PB, 978-1-58023-448-1 **$19.99**; HC, 978-1-58023-359-0 **$24.99**

The Divine Feminine in Biblical Wisdom Literature
Selections Annotated & Explained
Translation & Annotation by Rabbi Rami Shapiro
5½ x 8½, 240 pp, Quality PB, 978-1-59473-109-9 **$16.99**
(A book from SkyLight Paths, Jewish Lights' sister imprint)

The Quotable Jewish Woman
Wisdom, Inspiration & Humor from the Mind & Heart
Edited by Elaine Bernstein Partnow
6 x 9, 496 pp, Quality PB, 978-1-58023-236-4 **$19.99**

The Women's Haftarah Commentary
New Insights from Women Rabbis on the 54 Weekly Haftarah Portions, the 5 Megillot & Special Shabbatot
Edited by Rabbi Elyse Goldstein
Illuminates the historical significance of female portrayals in the Haftarah and the Five Megillot. 6 x 9, 560 pp, Quality PB, 978-1-58023-371-2 **$19.99**

The Women's Torah Commentary
New Insights from Women Rabbis on the 54 Weekly Torah Portions
Edited by Rabbi Elyse Goldstein
Over fifty women rabbis offer inspiring insights on the Torah, in a week-by-week format.
6 x 9, 496 pp, Quality PB, 978-1-58023-370-5 **$19.99**; HC, 978-1-58023-076-6 **$34.95**

See Passover for *The Women's Passover Companion: Women's Reflections on the Festival of Freedom* and *The Women's Seder Sourcebook: Rituals & Readings for Use at the Passover Seder.*

Inspiration

God of Me: Imagining God throughout Your Lifetime
By Rabbi David Lyon Helps you cut through preconceived ideas of God and dogmas that stifle your creativity when thinking about your personal relationship with God. 6 x 9, 176 pp, Quality PB, 978-1-58023-452-8 **$16.99**

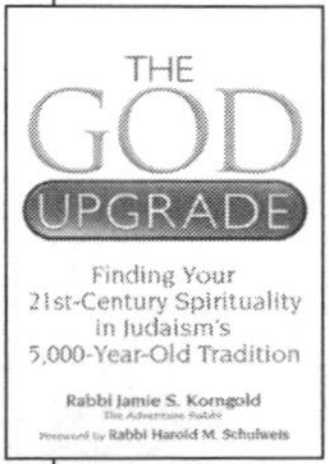

The God Upgrade: Finding Your 21st-Century Spirituality in Judaism's 5,000-Year-Old Tradition *By Rabbi Jamie Korngold; Foreword by Rabbi Harold M. Schulweis* A provocative look at how our changing God concepts have shaped every aspect of Judaism. 6 x 9, 176 pp, Quality PB, 978-1-58023-443-6 **$15.99**

The Seven Questions You're Asked in Heaven: Reviewing and Renewing Your Life on Earth *By Dr. Ron Wolfson* An intriguing and entertaining resource for living a life that matters. 6 x 9, 176 pp, Quality PB, 978-1-58023-407-8 **$16.99**

Happiness and the Human Spirit: The Spirituality of Becoming the Best You Can Be *By Rabbi Abraham J. Twerski, MD*
Shows you that true happiness is attainable once you stop looking outside yourself for the source. 6 x 9, 176 pp, Quality PB, 978-1-58023-404-7 **$16.99**; HC, 978-1-58023-343-9 **$19.99**

A Formula for Proper Living: Practical Lessons from Life and Torah
By Rabbi Abraham J. Twerski, MD 6 x 9, 144 pp, HC, 978-1-58023-402-3 **$19.99**

The Bridge to Forgiveness: Stories and Prayers for Finding God and Restoring Wholeness *By Rabbi Karyn D. Kedar* 6 x 9, 176 pp, Quality PB, 978-1-58023-451-1 **$16.99**

The Empty Chair: Finding Hope and Joy—Timeless Wisdom from a Hasidic Master, Rebbe Nachman of Breslov *Adapted by Moshe Mykoff and the Breslov Research Institute*
4 x 6, 128 pp, Deluxe PB w/ flaps, 978-1-879045-67-5 **$9.99**

The Gentle Weapon: Prayers for Everyday and Not-So-Everyday Moments—Timeless Wisdom from the Teachings of the Hasidic Master, Rebbe Nachman of Breslov
Adapted by Moshe Mykoff and S. C. Mizrahi, together with the Breslov Research Institute
4 x 6, 144 pp, Deluxe PB w/ flaps, 978-1-58023-022-3 **$9.99**

God Whispers: Stories of the Soul, Lessons of the Heart *By Rabbi Karyn D. Kedar*
6 x 9, 176 pp, Quality PB, 978-1-58023-088-9 **$15.95**

God's To-Do List: 103 Ways to Be an Angel and Do God's Work on Earth
By Dr. Ron Wolfson 6 x 9, 144 pp, Quality PB, 978-1-58023-301-9 **$16.99**

Jewish Stories from Heaven and Earth: Inspiring Tales to Nourish the Heart and Soul *Edited by Rabbi Dov Peretz Elkins* 6 x 9, 304 pp, Quality PB, 978-1-58023-363-7 **$16.99**

Life's Daily Blessings: Inspiring Reflections on Gratitude and Joy for Every Day, Based on Jewish Wisdom *By Rabbi Kerry M. Olitzky* 4½ x 6½, 368 pp, Quality PB, 978-1-58023-396-5 **$16.99**

Restful Reflections: Nighttime Inspiration to Calm the Soul, Based on Jewish Wisdom
By Rabbi Kerry M. Olitzky and Rabbi Lori Forman 4½ x 6½, 448 pp, Quality PB, 978-1-58023-091-9 **$15.95**

Sacred Intentions: Morning Inspiration to Strengthen the Spirit, Based on Jewish Wisdom
By Rabbi Kerry M. Olitzky and Rabbi Lori Forman 4½ x 6½, 448 pp, Quality PB, 978-1-58023-061-2 **$16.99**

Kabbalah/Mysticism

Jewish Mysticism and the Spiritual Life: Classical Texts, Contemporary Reflections *Edited by Dr. Lawrence Fine, Dr. Eitan Fishbane and Rabbi Or N. Rose*
Inspirational and thought-provoking materials for contemplation, discussion and action. 6 x 9, 256 pp, HC, 978-1-58023-434-4 **$24.99**

Ehyeh: A Kabbalah for Tomorrow
By Rabbi Arthur Green, PhD 6 x 9, 224 pp, Quality PB, 978-1-58023-213-5 **$18.99**

The Gift of Kabbalah: Discovering the Secrets of Heaven, Renewing Your Life on Earth
By Tamar Frankiel, PhD 6 x 9, 256 pp, Quality PB, 978-1-58023-141-1 **$16.95**

Seek My Face: A Jewish Mystical Theology *By Rabbi Arthur Green, PhD*
6 x 9, 304 pp, Quality PB, 978-1-58023-130-5 **$19.95**

Zohar: Annotated & Explained *Translation & Annotation by Dr. Daniel C. Matt; Foreword by Andrew Harvey* 5½ x 8½, 176 pp, Quality PB, 978-1-893361-51-5 **$15.99**
(A book from SkyLight Paths, Jewish Lights' sister imprint)

See also *The Way Into Jewish Mystical Tradition* in The Way Into... Series.

Meditation

Jewish Meditation Practices for Everyday Life
Awakening Your Heart, Connecting with God
By Rabbi Jeff Roth
Offers a fresh take on meditation that draws on life experience and living life with greater clarity as opposed to the traditional method of rigorous study.
6 x 9, 224 pp, Quality PB, 978-1-58023-397-2 **$18.99**

The Handbook of Jewish Meditation Practices
A Guide for Enriching the Sabbath and Other Days of Your Life
By Rabbi David A. Cooper Easy-to-learn meditation techniques.
6 x 9, 208 pp, Quality PB, 978-1-58023-102-2 **$16.95**

Discovering Jewish Meditation, 2nd Edition
Instruction & Guidance for Learning an Ancient Spiritual Practice
By Nan Fink Gefen, PhD 6 x 9, 208 pp, Quality PB, 978-1-58023-462-7 **$16.99**

Meditation from the Heart of Judaism
Today's Teachers Share Their Practices, Techniques, and Faith
Edited by Avram Davis 6 x 9, 256 pp, Quality PB, 978-1-58023-049-0 **$16.95**

Ritual/Sacred Practices

The Jewish Dream Book: The Key to Opening the Inner Meaning of Your Dreams *By Vanessa L. Ochs, PhD, with Elizabeth Ochs; Illus. by Kristina Swarner*
Instructions for how modern people can perform ancient Jewish dream practices and dream interpretations drawn from the Jewish wisdom tradition.
8 x 8, 128 pp, Full-color illus., Deluxe PB w/ flaps, 978-1-58023-132-9 **$16.95**

God in Your Body: Kabbalah, Mindfulness and Embodied Spiritual Practice
By Jay Michaelson
The first comprehensive treatment of the body in Jewish spiritual practice and an essential guide to the sacred.
6 x 9, 272 pp, Quality PB, 978-1-58023-304-0 **$18.99**

The Book of Jewish Sacred Practices: CLAL's Guide to Everyday & Holiday Rituals & Blessings *Edited by Rabbi Irwin Kula and Vanessa L. Ochs, PhD*
6 x 9, 368 pp, Quality PB, 978-1-58023-152-7 **$18.95**

Jewish Ritual: A Brief Introduction for Christians
By Rabbi Kerry M. Olitzky and Rabbi Daniel Judson
5½ x 8½, 144 pp, Quality PB, 978-1-58023-210-4 **$14.99**

The Rituals & Practices of a Jewish Life: A Handbook for Personal Spiritual Renewal *Edited by Rabbi Kerry M. Olitzky and Rabbi Daniel Judson*
6 x 9, 272 pp, Illus., Quality PB, 978-1-58023-169-5 **$18.95**

The Sacred Art of Lovingkindness: Preparing to Practice
By Rabbi Rami Shapiro 5½ x 8½, 176 pp, Quality PB, 978-1-59473-151-8 **$16.99**
(A book from SkyLight Paths, Jewish Lights' sister imprint)

Science Fiction/Mystery & Detective Fiction

Criminal Kabbalah: An Intriguing Anthology of Jewish Mystery & Detective Fiction *Edited by Lawrence W. Raphael; Foreword by Laurie R. King*
All-new stories from twelve of today's masters of mystery and detective fiction—sure to delight mystery buffs of all faith traditions.
6 x 9, 256 pp, Quality PB, 978-1-58023-109-1 **$16.95**

Mystery Midrash: An Anthology of Jewish Mystery & Detective Fiction
Edited by Lawrence W. Raphael; Preface by Joel Siegel
6 x 9, 304 pp, Quality PB, 978-1-58023-055-1 **$16.95**

Wandering Stars: An Anthology of Jewish Fantasy & Science Fiction
Edited by Jack Dann; Introduction by Isaac Asimov
6 x 9, 272 pp, Quality PB, 978-1-58023-005-6 **$18.99**

More Wandering Stars: An Anthology of Outstanding Stories of Jewish Fantasy and Science Fiction *Edited by Jack Dann; Introduction by Isaac Asimov*
6 x 9, 192 pp, Quality PB, 978-1-58023-063-6 **$16.95**